CW00543654

Warlords of Oman

Warlords of Oman was first published in 1967, but the action
is set in the fifties, and records some of the exciting events
leading to the resolution of international and local conflicts.
The security achieved was essential for the discovery of oil in
Oman after many years of frustration and disappointment.
The oil exports in the late sixties paved the way for
momentous change in a country that had until then been
virtually closed to the outside world. Under the government
of His Majesty, Sultan Qaboos, the country and its people
have prospered and changed out of all recognition. Oman has
been transformed into a haven of peace and prosperity. While
still preserving its ancient heritage, culture and natural
beauty, the Sultanate has become a thoroughly modern
welfare state in a remarkably short space of time.

WARLORDS
OF OMAN

P. S. ALLFREE

ROBERT HALE · LONDON

For my wife

© P.S. Allfree 1967
First published in Great Britain 1967
Paperback edition 2008

ISBN 978 0 7090 8600 0

Robert Hale Limited
Clerkenwell House
Clerkenwell Green
London EC1R 0HT

www.halebooks.com

The right of P.S. Allfree to be identified as author of
this work has been asserted by him in accordance
with the Copyright, Designs and Patents Act 1988

A catalogue record for this book is available from the British Library

10 9 8 7 6 5 4 3 2

Printed by the MPG Books Group, Bodmin and King's Lynn

FOREWORD

The events recorded in this memoir describe a very different country from the Sultanate of Oman that we know today. Muscat & Oman, as it was then known, was a part of the world almost completely off the beaten track. Entry was restricted for foreigners and there was very little communication with the outside world. Few books about Oman or the Gulf States had been published when *Warlords of Oman* first appeared in print. Thus it soon became required reading for students, diplomats and visitors interested in the history of Arabia.

The story begins with the dispute over the ownership of the Buraimi Oasis that became an international cause célèbre in 1952. Until the search for oil was intensified after the Second World War, vast tracts of Arabia were not properly demarcated. Tribal disputes had to be resolved and boundaries drawn up by treaties and oil concessions. The only law and order was enforced by a handful of tribal guards. Military and police forces all had to be raised from scratch. The author describes the recruitment and training of the Trucial Oman Levies in the first part of the book. The Levies would later become the Trucial Oman Scouts and were the forerunners of the Abu Dhabi Defence Force that we know today. With the ongoing search for oil in Oman, the Sultan also needed security forces for the protection of the industry and its personnel. The author describes the early basic tactics and operations of the units that have now been expanded with an impressive array of modern equipment into the Sultan's Armed Forces.

Although much has been written since about the momentous events of more than half a century ago, *Warlords of Oman* remains a classic of Arabian travel and experience. It is full of lively descriptions of people and places. Its pages abound with delightful scenes of local colour, lively encounters, fascinating characters, a sense of humour and exciting incidents. The story is remarkable for a lightness of touch and an absence of romanticism. The difficulties and hardships faced by those involved are set down without exaggeration and make the modern reader, accustomed to all the benefits and technical innovations found in today's affluent society wonder at their stamina and resistance.

In 1969 when I was about to leave for work in Oman, I bought a copy of *Warlords of Oman*. Following the story closely and knowing some of its characters, I very much regretted that I had arrived too late to be a part of such an era of adventure and excitement. I regret that I only had the opportunity of meeting Philip Allfree very briefly, although our paths nearly crossed in the army and later in Yemen. Having always admired his writing, it now gives me much satisfaction to see *Warlords of Oman*, which is dedicated to his widow Audrey, in print again.

Julian Paxton

CONTENTS

The publication of a paperback edition of
Warlords of Oman has been made possible by a
grant from the Anglo-Omani Society as part of
its remit to bring the history and culture of
Oman to a wider audience

ILLUSTRATIONS

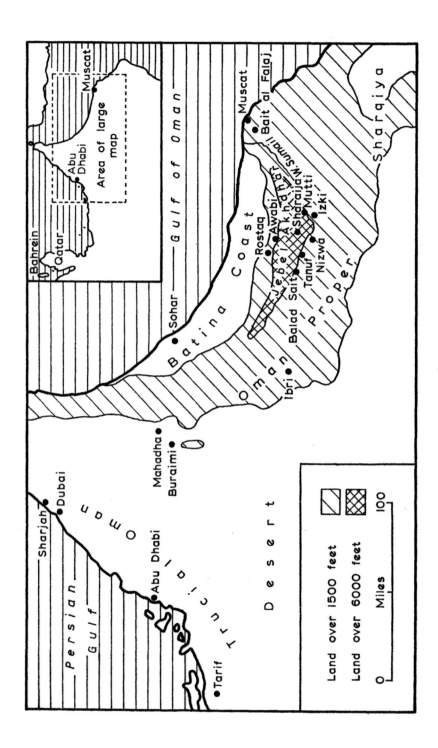

1

OASIS IN QUARANTINE

T H E scarlet brigadier turned to a map of the Middle East on the wall of his office, waved his hand vaguely over it and brought it down spread-fingered to cover half the Arabian Peninsula.

"There," he said prodigiously, "is the Buraimi Oasis."

Then he turned to me and clapped a paw on my shoulder. "It's a hard life, me boy," he made a noise like *hrrumph,* "but a jolly well worth while job of work. Good luck."

This impressive interview took place in late 1953, in the General Headquarters of our Middle East forces, which in those days had yet to be evicted from the Suez Canal. Its antecedents were these : first, I had spent nearly a year as one of several thousand soldiers penned behind the barbed wire of an enormous dump of military stores and Army rubbish called Tel el Kebir, trying unsuccessfully to guard it against the fathomless cunning of Egyptian thieves; and, secondly, disturbing news had been seeping out from the virtually unexplored depths of eastern Arabia. It is not surprising that the brightly-coloured brigadier was unable to brief me more thoroughly about the task, although he may have been one of the best-informed men in G.H.Q. at the time. Trucial Oman—the Pirate Coast—the Sultanate of Muscat—were scarcely even names except on the larger maps, and the idea of British military involvement there was about as remote as in the Galapagos Islands.

But endless guards and foot inspections had dispelled my illusions of military glamour, and the tiny notice in Army orders soliciting volunteers for the "Trucial Oman Levies" had aroused my curiosity if not my enthusiasm. Whatever they were, I thought, they must be a change from that; so I volunteered. Not even my brigadier was able to tell me what these Levies were, or why; I had to find that out for myself—and they got me out from behind the wire.

Arabia looks like the head of a rhinoceros, with its nose poking into the Arabian Sea and its horn jutting up towards Persia. Its ear is a flat oil-producing sand-spit called Qatar. Most of the animal is Saudi Arabia, and much of that is the great desert known as the Empty Quarter, but all the way from Qatar round to Aden is a string of wildly independent but determinedly sovereign States of which the largest are big enough to be shown separately on the map and the smallest are merely isolated fishing villages. A number of these minor nations are strung along the Persian Gulf from the ear of the rhinoceros to the tip of its horn; in the nineteenth century this strip of moon-like litoral was called the Pirate Coast after the favourite occupation and principal livelihood of the inhabitants, but a series of naval bombardments by the Maritime Powers and one or two landing parties of blue-jackets persuaded the chieftains to bind themselves and their successors in a perpetual truce with each other and with the rest of mankind. The pirate coast then became known as the Trucial Coast, Trucial States, or Trucial Oman (the name is derivative of "truce"), and under the usually wise tutelage of a succession of resident British Political Agents these principalities withdrew from history for well over a hundred years.

The snout of the rhinoceros and some extent inland below its horn is a very different country, which in the years following World War II was still being only tentatively prodded and poked by explorers who travelled disguised as bedouin and avoided meeting anybody. This is Oman, sometimes called Oman Proper as distinct from the Trucial variety; it is a populous and fertile region with abundant water from cloudy mountains, verdant valleys, and a people noted among the other Arabs for religious fanaticism and a hatred of their fellow men. It is, however, something of an oasis in an otherwise desert land; and moreover there were in those days whispers of oil companies casting seductive eyes in its direction.

Oman is virtually an island, surrounded on two sides by the ocean and on the other two by an even more formidable sea— the billowing sands of the Empty Quarter. For this reason the country had developed over the centuries a distinct air of not belonging to the rest of Arabia, and had been studiously ignored by the world in its turn—apart from Albuquerque the predatory Portuguese, a dynasty of American missionaries, and the inevitable British builders of Empire.

There is only one practicable land route from the outside world, from the coastal towns of the Gulf and from the inhabited parts of Saudi Arabia, and this is along the coast and down the edge of the mountains where there is a strip of territory which the hungry sands have not yet swallowed up. On this route there is one vital oasis, and the name of that oasis is Buraimi.

Buraimi was in those pre-oil days a cluster of seven villages mouldering peacefully between the mountains and the desert, about eighty miles inland from the Persian Gulf ports of Dubai and Sharjah (both of these harbours ranked as sovereign States). The villages of Buraimi were for the most part clusters of crumbling mud huts huddled together to form almost a continuous heap, like yellow boxes cemented together and covered in dust. Each group was surrounded by a dark-green lake of date-groves, and each had its tottering mud castle which the winds and occasional rains of centuries had eroded so that they seemed to extrude from the sandy soil like monstrous ant-hills.

On the western side the desert was remorselessly encroaching, flooding in from the oceans of sand in the hinterland of the sub-continent, till the foremost waves lapped at the walls of the outer villages and isolated buildings and overspilt and flowed, an irresistible tide, in between the settlements.

Such was this vital market and watering-place on the only land route to the misty hills of Oman two hundred miles to the south. Like many places with a similar geography, Buraimi's history was one of repeated changes of flag. In the last century it had for a while been tributary to the Wahhabi chiefs of what

13

is now Saudi Arabia, but latterly it had been split between the rulers of Oman proper and Abu Dhabi (another Trucial State). Three of the larger villages belonged to whoever happened to be ruling Oman at the time, and the rest to the Abu Dhabi Sheikh.

Until twentieth-century history burst upon Buraimi so rudely in the early 1950s, life there was as it had been since it was first settled. The people wore the dress of Oman, a calf-length gown and a coloured Kashmir shawl wrapped like a swashbuckling turban about the head; they wore a decorated dagger across the belly, in a belt stuffed with cartridges for the Martini Henry rifle they carried from puberty. They never shaved. For all but a very few, the only thing in their lives they owed to modern science was a hurricane lamp and the paraffin to feed it; for all but a few, Europe was another part of Arabia a bit further away than Baghdad, and Europeans were an odd-coloured Arab tribe who had yet to be converted to Islam. To a few intrepid explorers, Buraimi was the starting point—the last piece of *terra cognita*—before launching into the desolate seas of the desert and the unknown mysteries of Oman and the Green Mountains. To the rest of mankind Buraimi was not even a name.

Then one famous day of 1952 blitzkrieg came to Buraimi. A motorized column came incredibly out of the west, where there was nothing but waves of sand for six or seven hundred miles. The column had soldiers. Before anybody knew what was happening the leader, a man named Turki bin Abdullah bin Ataishan, announced to the astonished people that he was their Governor, appointed by none other than His Majesty King Abdulaziz Ibn Saud. . . .

There followed a period of immense confusion, political and military. The only forces at the disposal of the Sheikh of Abu Dhabi were his own armed tribesmen; those at the fingertips of the British Government, which was supposed to be the Protector of the area, were a small local military police force of some fifty men stationed at Sharjah under a British gentleman commander; the representative of Oman had a handful of bellicose but ineffective ceremonial guards. Turki made rapid progress in winning over the Oman part of Buraimi, and also a major tribe of

14

mountaineers, by the liberal use of money, but the Sheikh of Abu Dhabi had a redoubtable representative resident in his part of the oasis named Zaid who by virtue of his own enormous prestige and influence kept the infection from becoming a plague in that part of the area.

The British Government reacted by flying in Arab troops from Aden, who were swiftly involved in some battles, particularly against the dissident tribe in the hills; and the Sultan of Muscat mustered a formidable force of many thousands of his subjects and collected them on the coast north of his capital where there was a pass through the mountains to Buraimi. This horde was poised to hurl itself through the hills and sweep Turki and his Saudis back into the desert whence they had come—and if they had succeeded most of what follows for the next decade would never have happened. But at the eleventh hour Authority in the shape of His Britannic Majesty's Consul General arrived, breathless from Muscat, with a veto. It was feared in London that incalculable disasters might result from the use of force, whereas the gentler weapons of diplomacy were unlikely to cause any embarrassment in Whitehall. So the Sultan submitted, dismissed his array, and retired to his palace, there to wait and see; if all was well, then he would be content; but if the appeasement policies of Whitehall were to have the effect that such policies had been known to have elsewhere. . . .

It is I think fair to say that the Sultan never forgave Britain for turning him back.

Nor, to be fair, did the British Government allow its own forces to be used offensively against the invaders. They settled down to besiege them; not primarily with the idea of reducing Turki by famine, but to seal him off from the rest of the human race; those he had already suborned with his generosity, the inhabitants of the Sultan's villages, were left to bask under the green and white flag of King Ibn Saud, but a cordon was thrown around them to ensure that the contagion spread no further.

This quarantine became the fixed policy of the British authorities. Minute care was taken to ensure that no offence was done to Turki and his men; he was not allowed out, but we were not allowed in. As far as I know, the only people from our side to visit Turki at home were two erratic British servicemen who arrived in the oasis by night and drove up to his stronghold under the mistaken impression that it was ours. The gates opened; they were welcomed inside; the gates closed behind them. It was some time before anybody discovered where they were. When the Political Agency found out, they sent a severely-worded ultimatum to the effect that Turki was to release his guests by a certain hour, or else. . . . Turki allowed the ultimatum to expire by a comfortable and conspicuous margin, and then graciously dismissed the two bewildered Tommies, who had been well treated and can have had no idea of the hideous fate from which we had tried to save them.

The Arab troops from Aden were shortly needed in their own country, and emergency measures were taken to give the British Political Agent some punch of his own. The nucleus was the exiguous gendarmerie of fifty men known as the Trucial Oman Levies. Gangs of discharged soldiers from Aden were dug out of the back streets and freighted up to Sharjah; first one, then another, British Army officer found himself sent to the same place, to the marvellous surprise of at least one of them who thought he had volunteered for something quite different; the Adenese ex-soldiers were enlisted into the Trucial Oman Levies, placed under command of the dismayed officers, and packed off to besiege Turki bin Ataishan.

These soldiers had unmistakable advantages. They were trained men, needing only uniforms and weapons to be ready for the field. The emergency made them welcome. However, they had defects, which became more and more apparent—with at least one tragic consequence—and these defects ultimately outweighed their advantages and we got rid of them. For one thing, they had in many cases been discharged from the Aden forces dishonourably and had learnt no more honour in the alleys and bazaars where they lurked until enticed out into the open air by the generous offer of re-enlistment in Sharjah. Not to put too fine a point on it, there was more than a fair share of criminals. For another thing, they had not the slightest interest in whether Turki or the Sultan or the Sheikh of Abu Dhabi lived or died, and they owed no allegiance whatever to the Political Agent. They were mercenaries pure and simple, and a mercenary has only one purpose in taking up arms—to get what he can out of it.

There was not a great deal these mercenaries could gain in the way of legitimate loot, perched in their lookout posts and picquets around Buraimi and severely forbidden to set so much as a toe inside Turki's sanctuary. They found, however, that they had one commodity which they could sell for good cash to their supposed enemies—and a commodity which their own officers obligingly replaced as fast as they disposed of it. This was their ammunition. They would fire off a few rounds into the night, from their guardpost; their officer or sergeant-major would hear the alarming sound and rush out to investigate. In prompt military fashion they reported : "Intruders attempting to pass the blockade; failed to stop when challenged three times; fire opened and exchanged; we expended—let's see—eighty-seven rounds." The eighty-seven replacement rounds represented a net profit of probably eighty, retailing at one or two rupees apiece.

This ruse quickly became sorely obvious to the British officer in command, but it was hard to obtain legal proof of the activity—it is scarcely fair to require troops on active service to collect their empty cartridge cases after every engagement, as if they were on the ranges. But in due course the commander, whose name was Otto Thwaites and who was wildly eccentric but highly regarded by those who knew him, decided that he had enough to warrant the arrest of the directors of this lucrative business. He set out in his Land-Rover, accompanied by the regimental sergeant-major who was a Jordanian, the medical officer who was on loan from the Royal Air Force, and a British sergeant of R.E.M.E. who happened to be in Buraimi for technical reasons and was invited along to see the fun.

The Levies' picquet posts were well sited, to cover all possible approaches to Turki's lair. The Land-Rover with its valuable load drove towards one of them and was at once enveloped in a murderous cross-fire from Otto's own troops. Otto was killed; so was the R.S.M., and the doctor. The sergeant was wounded but he managed to drive the vehicle with its tragic burden out of danger and back to the company headquarters.

Reaction from authority was swift. A new company was mobilized in Sharjah and sent down to disarm the mutineers and assume the cordon. The murderers melted into the desert but were picked up by Zaid's men and handed over to the Levies. They spent about eight months cooped up in a jail the size of a privy, in Sharjah, while a lengthy diplomatic wrangle wound itself to a conclusion about who had jurisdiction over them: the British Government, whose subjects they had assassinated and in whose service they were; the Sultan of Muscat, on whose territory the crime had been committed; and for all I know, the Sheikh of Abu Dhabi and the Governor of Aden as well. In the fullness of time they were handed over to the Sultan and committed for a number of years in his prison.

This was the situation in November 1953, when the scarlet brigadier wished me luck in so cordial a manner. So remote was the area, and so confused the situation, that he can be forgiven for not having more precise information to offer me; but the tour of duty was only eighteen months, and eighteen months in hell itself would at least have been a change from the futile guard duties in the wire-girt dump of Tel el Kebir.

I was even looking forward to it.

2

A SHOWER OF SANDALS

SHARJAH was not the most unattractive place in Arabia. Worse was a solitary well in the Empty Quarter called Sanau, a sulphurous pit which could be smelt for miles around, sunk amid white gypsum hills which gleamed like icebergs in the desert sun; there was a miserable town on the Arabian Sea called Ghaidha, with flies so numerous and so hungry that they clustered greedily on your forkful of food before you could close your mouth on it, where every house was fortified against its neighbour and fear and hatred lay heavy on the air.

But Sharjah, in 1954, came a fairly long way down the list. It was a huddle of little grey hovels, made of dried palm-leaves woven into shaggy mats, sprawled over a square mile or so of the pallid yellow sand-dunes and murky white salt-marsh which make up the Persian Gulf coast in this corner. Lurking in the midst of this shanty town was the Sheikh's palace, a crumbling structure painted blue and white like Gorgonzola cheese, with a cannon outside its front door used for public floggings. The town had as many dogs as human beings, and both classes of inhabitant had similar ideas of sanitation—from which the prevailing smell of Sharjah derived.

This unpleasant place was my first landfall in Arabia. In those days it was still supposed to be the premier town of the Trucial States, although it had long been overtaken by its more forceful neighbour Dubai. It was then the seat of the British Political

19

Agent, and it had the only aerodrome in the territory, a Royal Air Force station and a civil airport.

The airport buildings were known as The Fort, and a fort they were, dating from the days not so long past when passengers, crews, and administrative paraphernalia were protected from marauding nomads by a stone-built castle with a steel gate and turrets with slits for machine-guns. By the time I arrived, civilization had come to Sharjah : the steel doors no longer slid, the loopholes were vacant. One relic of the great days remained, however, and I expect still remains to this day. This was an old man with a gun who lived on a bench just inside the gateway, on permanent sentry-go. I, for one, never went into the Fort at any time of night or day without seeing him in his place. By day he sat on his bench, and by night he slept on it, and he had his meals where he sat. I have never seen a more contented man.

At Sharjah, too, was the headquarters of the Trucial Oman Levies, who were lodgers of the Royal Air Force. The R.A.F. station was something of a slum, despite the often heroic efforts of its officers—who, mercifully for them, were only posted there for a few months at a time. It was a compound of low tin-roofed huts, each with its clanking air-conditioner which looked and sounded like a steam traction-engine and extracted from the moisture-laden atmosphere a steady stream of water before delivering a breathable but insipid breeze to the inmates. Without these machines life would have been intolerable in the summer. In that climate, natives from inland suffered prickly heat and went down with heatstroke; on especially bad days there was a thick fog until the morning was well advanced, muffling the place in a soggy blanket of warm steam.

Our water was similarly an artificial product. Although the town of Sharjah had a small number of shallow wells, offering up a strongly-flavoured liquid in limited quantities (which was sold in the streets at so much a gallon from donkeys laden with old paraffin-tins), the R.A.F. preferred to make their own from the brine which underlay the salt-marsh on which they lived. Distilled water is so tasteless as to be positively nasty and we seldom took it without some flavouring, generally alcoholic. In the suffocating heat our drinking was methodical, deliberate and huge—certainly among us Levy officers; as I remember, the R.A.F. were more temperate, but they seldom emerged from their artificial indoor climate. For us, the combination of almost insufferable weather, a task that drove us mad with frustration, nothing else whatever to do—and horrible drinking water— worked its alchemy on our way of life. Every Sunday the entire corps of officers (about half a dozen) repaired to the Fort where round after round of frosty beer was followed by uncountable circuits of pink gin. Our booze left the body via the sweat glands, by-passing the bladder entirely.

Later on that year the Levies took over the Political Agent's house in Sharjah town, when the Foreign Office had recognized that Dubai was vastly larger and more metropolitan and built themselves comfortable new quarters there. Our new mess, a primitive and beetle-infested building of coral rock, had the advantage that we were together in our own home instead of being lodgers with the boys in blue; but this togetherness was bought at a price. We were right on the seafront, and the clammy atmosphere overlay us like a hot damp pall. In midsummer we tried sleeping on the roof; at around four in the morning we might finally drop off, after a night of squirming on spongy mattresses that were saturated with dew and our own sweat— but we had to be up at five in order to get any work done before it grew too hot, which it did at about ten. The only way, we quickly found, to get a reasonable amount of sleep per twenty-four hours was to soak up enough gin at lunch-time to anaesthetize us until the evening. That way, too, we could ignore the coral-flies—minute insects which bred in the streets of Sharjah and had a liking for human ears and nostrils, and any other orifices to which they might gain access.

The headquarters of the Levies in those days were little better than the shanty town of Sharjah itself. In later years they were rebuilt and smartened up, with whitewashed stones and all, but then it was a ramshackle eye-sore of hutments put together out of date-palm matting, tied together—quite literally—with string. When it rained the whole barracks leaked like a sponge, and, like a sponge, went on leaking long after the rain had stopped.

In this uninspiring environment a devoted handful of officers strove to build an army.

After the mutiny and murders in Buraimi it was decided to send the Adenese riff-raff back to their homes eight hundred miles away, and make of the Trucial Oman Levies a real native force. There were no regrets, only a certain amount of apprehension at the size of the task. The local tribesmen were, on the whole, well-disposed to the British Government and many of them were fanatically devoted to Sheikh Zaid of Buraimi; the problem was, not to recruit them, but to train them, and sufficiently rapidly to enable us to deport the Adenese before they did something frightful again. As I was the most spare of the half-dozen officers in Sharjah—having wrestled for a few weeks with the motor transport, ignorant of the difference between a clutch plate and a spark gap, and having failed spectacularly to keep the odd collection of jalopies which masqueraded as our motor transport in going condition—the task of training our willing but wild recruits fell upon me.

We had six weeks in which to transform bearded brigands into trained troops: cameleers into riflemen, a desert barbarian into Number Two on the Bren. In fact it was done. Perhaps some of the company commanders to whom these transmogrified bedouin were posted found them a bit rough-cast; I did so myself when later on I was put in charge of a company of my own ex-pupils: but they were soldiers, albeit imperfect. The inspiration for this job came from Colonel Eric Johnson, whose peculiar sympathy for the Arabs did more to tide the Levies over this teething period than any other single factor. A lean, ascetic teetotaller, Johnson was at times a martinet—with officers and soldiers whom he expected to know their business; unlike some British officers who "got on well with Arabs" he was neither a peculiar outsider nor was he one of those whose lack of military quality could only be dissimulated in unnatural conditions like ours. He made almost no effort at all even to learn Arabic. But he had a way of softening the impact of military life to these free-running men of the desert, at a time when a less flexible attitude would merely have dried up the stream of recruits and scattered those we had to the four winds. For all the necessary harshness of a recruit's first days in uniform, with Johnson they accepted it. There would come a time when the army, and the way we soldiered, were familiar enough in the Trucial States for more conventional attitudes to prevail, but Johnson was the man for the season.

One of my first shocks when presented with a band of these raw ruffians was how badly they could shoot. The proverbial hawk-eyed tribesman with his unerring marksmanship is a myth; in Arabia, anyway. There were times, later, when I was grateful that this is so (perhaps I was lucky, perhaps there are others who have as good reason to dispute this—I can only record my experience); but when the bad shots were on my side and I was charged with the task of making them better, it was a disappointment. On the rifle range they thought it a triumph if they hit the target at all. It took some patience to explain the significance of the concentric circles drawn on the four-foot square : if the man had nine holes out of ten somewhere on the frame, he was content.

But the most fascinating phenomena took place on the parade ground. Any British Army drill-sergeant commands a graphic vocabulary to describe his gaggle of recruits when they first appear before him; but a band of desert Arabs newly arrived in barracks is a nightmare. At least the European recruit has some vague, atavistic notion of what is involved. He has seen pictures of soldiers, he has seen soldiers in the flesh; however awkward he may be, his sergeant does not have to plough completely virgin soil. But we did. The whole concept of soldiering as we do it, of discipline, of drill, was something as alien to these willing lads as nuclear physics. We would carefully place them in line and enjoin silence; they would break up into little knots and discuss their impressions. The instructor would demonstrate a drill movement; the recruits would chat about what they had just seen, applauding or criticizing. On the order "Quick march" the whole group would amble raggedly forward—the Arabic word of command was "forward march", luckily, otherwise they would each have chosen his own direction.

I was beginning, too, to come up against the all-pervading

23

sense of the Supreme Being which is so marked a characteristic of the undebauched Arab, and which was to stretch our patience to a scream. The first impact was this : to every order we gave, the reply was no smart salute and "Yes sir", but a roll of the eyes to heaven and a murmured "If God wills". "Report to me after the parade, Abdullah"—"If God wills". "Fall in for weapon training at eleven o'clock"—"If God wills." "Pull your stomach in"—"Take three days C.B."—the reply was the same, with a regularity which could drive a man used to more usual responses to the bottle. Hence, in part, our marathon Sunday sessions at the Fort. The poor soldier was not being insolent; what he was trying to say, as succinctly as he could, was that provided the Almighty approved he intended to carry the order out; but should he be struck dead, or the Last Trump blow, then he was not to be blamed.

Slowly, miraculously, as days went by, the twenty or so in-dividuals—who might spread in age from fourteen to forty, there was no way of knowing within ten years or so—took shape as a squad. Each day, one less was out of step; each day, one less tried to slope arms on the wrong shoulder. One of the last ob-stacles was the sandal barrier. Not being used to wearing any-thing on them, they had feet a different shape to those of people who do, and they had enormous difficulty in managing the heavy sandals we supplied them and obliged them to wear. At the be-ginning they shed their sandals on the march all over the parade ground. An about turn was accompanied by a shower of shoes shied into the air by their happy foot-stamping. The drill parades were interrupted every twenty minutes for them to collect their footwear. But even this was overcome, and by the fourth week or so we had a recognizable squad of soldiers; at the end of the sixth their passing-out parade was a joy to those who remembered what they were like a month and a half before.

A difficulty of a different kind was rather harder to defeat, and caused many hard words between ourselves and our kind hosts, the Royal Air Force. I have touched on the sanitary arrange-ments in Sharjah. The fact of the matter is that the Arab, in his natural state, is a man of the desert and problems of sanitation are of no more concern to him than they are to his camel. This is all right in the desert; it is fine, in a hot dry climate, for a small village with plenty of empty space around it—an Arab village smells no worse than an English one. In a crowded slum-town like Sharjah, where the air is heavy and dank, the thing begins to make itself noticed. However, the Arab is a man of tradition, and the traditions of the desert are that you never leave your droppings anywhere near where anybody else has; furthermore, the habits of the village make it an unspeakably disgusting thing to leave them inside a building.

The tussle we had, with these inborn prejudices on the one hand and the R.A.F. Commanding Officer's concern for his camp on the other, can be imagined. Our men had latrines, as a matter of course, but to get them to use them—something just as repugnant to them as the reverse would be to us—was not the least of our struggles in rebuilding the Trucial Oman Levies.

Meanwhile I was gradually discovering Arabia, and finding it—as my acquaintance developed—less and less like its popular image projected from a hundred books of traveller's tales, romance, and combinations of the two.

Soon after I arrived, while my eyes were still wide with wonder, the Arab officers' mess threw a party. This was my introduction to Arab feasts, about which much has already been written but which remains about the most unappetizing way of presenting food that can ever have been devised. Only one sort of meat is thought worthy of an Arab feast, and that is the flesh of the goat. Mutton is considered very poor cheer. The Biblical separation of sheep from goats is not what we think : in the lands of its origin, goats are the valuable creatures and sheep merely perambulating providers of wool—which is not as hard-wearing as goat-hair, either.

So we had goat : more precisely, we had *a* goat, complete but for its skin and hooves and horns, divided into four or five major portions and innumerable lesser pieces of entrail and other interior parts, reposing atop a mound of rice on a great round dish. On top of the whole pile was the goat's head, eyes and all. And here is another fallacy of fiction—and non-fiction—about Arabia. Not once in all the years I spent, in all the hundreds of times I shared an Arab's goat, was I ever offered an eye. I know of people who have eaten eyes, out of bravado—but they had to ask for them.

The feasters sit on the floor around the dish and partake with their bare hands. The host uses both hands to rend the haunches and shoulders into manageable portions, which he distributes to the guests, plonking a fistful of meat in front of each. The technique of eating is to scoop up a handful of rice together with a morsel of meat, using only one hand; squeeze it until the grease runs out between the fingers and the mass coheres into a globular lump; open the mouth, and flick it inside with the thumb. This takes a lot of practice. Most Europeans trying to manage an Arab meal make a mess as disgusting as a child trying for the first time to cope with knife and fork, the mess being on the floor and on their faces. Over the years I evolved a means of avoiding eating anything at all—reserving my appetite for my own diet—while appearing to feast hugely. With bunched fist I would poke a dent in the mound of rice in front of me, pretending to scoop but in fact only compressing, every now and then carrying the empty fist to my mouth and poking in an imaginary gobbet. The pieces of meat placed before me could be buried in the rice by this same process, as fast as they arrived. By the end of the meal I had a large hole in my rice, all my meat had gone . . . the only thing remaining was to summon up a well-rounded belch, and my host was gratified.

There was little variation on this theme all the way up or down the social scale. At a banquet given by the ruler of one of the Trucial States, there would be several goats on several dishes; there might be little saucers of tinned fruit; and the meal might be climaxed by the handing round of incense and the sprinkling of rose-water. At a small outpost of the army, or a poor man's house, the rice would be more meagre and there would be clouds of flies—even more than in the ruler's palace—but the goat would still be there in his place of honour on top. I have known exceptions, however. Once when visiting a very remote outpost, set for some reason in the midst of some sand dunes, I was offered—and prevailed upon to eat, my technique being then in its infancy—a dish with pieces of gristly flesh which I was led to believe to be rabbit. Only afterwards did I catch sight of a severed head like a young tyrannosaurus and a spiky tail like a species of cactus—the beast, which by now was stirring protestingly around inside me, had been a monitor lizard.

Travel in the Trucial States in those days was a nightmare. Even the few miles from Sharjah to Dubai could end in disaster; the road was a dozen miles long and about six miles wide, being merely an expanse of salty bog with a treacherous crust which would change its nature capriciously with the tide or the state of the moon—we never really tied it down. The sea had a way of poking inlets into what we had thought to be as firm a surface as asphalt.

Two bibulous gentlemen were once travelling this road after a convivial evening. The one who was driving had his foot hard to the floorboards and the engine was singing its highest note— top speed was always possible on this stretch. But for some reason his passenger became nervous, and asked him to slow down— "Not on your life," said the driver, hunched over the wheel like some Fangio. After a few more protests the passenger said, "Very well then, I'm getting out". He was told not to be stupid, at a speed of perhaps seventy miles an hour, but to the driver's horror his companion calmly opened the door and stepped out into the night. The man behind the wheel looked out of his window—he was still driving at full speed—and saw his friend standing placidly outside the vehicle, lighting a cigarette . . . even then it was a little while before he realized that he was down to his axles in wet slush, with his wheels spinning merrily as they had been for the last ten minutes.

Everything conspired against four-wheeled traffic. It was not only the condition of our vehicles—a motley assortment of wartime relics and travel-weary scrap; it was not only our drivers, who had an unhappy and sometimes fatal knack of turning turtle on the most perfectly flat terrain. Nor was it only the heat, which vaporized the petrol before it could reach the engine, nor the humid fogs which short-circuited the ignition. Our more inventive drivers cured both these ills with a piece of rag, in the first case soaked in water and wrapped round the fuel-pipe, in the second case soaked in petrol, ignited, and used as a flaming brand to dry the machine out.

But the whole geography of the place was in arms against us. The only road to Buraimi was a mere hundred miles long but we allowed up to twenty-four hours for it because of a four-mile barrier of sand. We had to time our arrival at this narrow obstacle for dawn, when the sand was cool and moist. We let almost all the air out of the tyres, so that they squatted down fatly on the ground; then bottom gear and throttle to the floor would, we hoped, take us roaring and grinding up the first slope. If it did not, we must stop and slide all the way back down again—hoping the vehicle would not slip and turn over—and then take another run at it. The urgent task was to maintain momentum—if we stopped in the middle there was a long way to push—but sometimes a wheel spun round while the flattened tyre stayed put so the valve was ripped out with a pop. Civilian lorries used to make this journey too, but never without a full cargo of passengers who virtually carried the truck over this stretch.

The coast road had its own charming character. It was hundreds of miles of salt marsh, flat and white as an ice-rink, dry enough in summer when the track became corrugated as if it had logs across it every three feet or so, and wet enough in winter to engulf a stationary vehicle to the floorboards—so here, as in the sand, one just kept going with a prayer on the lips. Any attempt to detour from the water-filled ruts on to the tempting virgin flats was punished by a sinking feeling.

But meanwhile the sands were running out for Turki and his men, comfortably besieged by our uncomfortable picquets. The King in Riyadh had agreed to submit to arbitration. The case would be argued in Geneva; meanwhile, Turki with his henchmen would pull out from his satrapy, and we would call off our soldiers. Buraimi was declared a neutral zone. For fifteen miles around, no Saudi nor Abu Dhabi nor Omani nor British influence would operate. A small police force provided half by the Saudis and half by the Trucial Oman Levies, with one Saudi and one British officer in joint charge, was left behind in complete isolation as the opposing powers withdrew.

A Shower of Sandals

Turki's departure was conducted with decorum but with one final snook cocked at Her Britannic Majesty to add to the incident of the two wandering soldiers. His troops were to have been escorted to the borders of Saudi Arabia by a detachment of ours; but he maintained forcefully that as Buraimi itself was an integral part of that kingdom he was already within those borders, and needed no escort. When the escort was tactfully downgraded to the status of a guiding party through the sands he said that as it was all his own native land he could do very well without guides too. There was a minor diplomatic crisis. As Duty Officer in Sharjah I made numerous trips to Dubai to consult the Political Agent. In the end the P.A. accepted that Turki felt more strongly about the matter than he did, and the garrison was allowed to depart unescorted and unguided—the way, in fact, it had come. The next we heard of Turki was that he was safely home, proving his point.

So the Saudis departed. The Levies established a military post on the edge of the fifteen mile circle. Meanwhile Sharjah still steamed like a Turkish bath; my recruits still shed their sandals in the August sun. Shortly, however, my sojourn in the relative luxury of H.Q. was to end, and I was to find out how really uncomfortable life could be. I was put in charge of a company of my own products, and spent many months with them as my companions in various remote and unlovely outposts.

3

MIRE AND MUTINY

"AND who are you?"

A small bearded Arab had hopped into my office like a flea.

"Gunpowder," he said.

I was mustering my company for taking them to our western outpost where they were to protect the oil company against the evil Turki.

I must have mis-heard him.

"What is your job?" I tried again.

"Gunpowder."

In this peculiar way began my association with Gunpowder Joe, medical orderly extraordinary. He bore the title as an honorific; it was really his pronunciation of the old military term "compounder" for dispenser or medical orderly. He turned up with a huge laundry-basket packed with rolls of cotton wool, splints, and bottles of nostrums for loosening or consolidating the bowels.

Then there was Epstein, a very black African with moustaches more like Sancho Panza than anybody else; but somehow the character of the great sculptor seemed to suit him best. He was a vehicle mechanic, and perhaps it was the way he set upon an intransigent lump of machinery and transformed it into a living thing that inspired his nickname. He had a way of leaping on top of an inert vehicle, twining his arms and feet (full of spanners and screwdrivers) around it and even inside it, in almost a symbolic tableau of begetting life, that seldom failed to strike the vital spark from the most desperately broken down junk. As with Gunpowder Joe, we dug deep down into natural springs for some of our specialists in those primitive days.

Two or three of the ordinary soldiers stood out from the face-less ranks, too. There was a very small boy who had arrived in Sharjah, half-naked and panting like a hare after a hard chase; he managed to complete the enlistment process just in time before the son of one of the local noblesse arrived in furious pursuit, claiming the child as his own. At first we thought that the re-lationship was of blood, but it soon appeared that it was well outside the limits of consanguinity and in fact would have been perfectly legitimate but for the coincidence of sex. We kept the boy, and the princeling departed frustrated and tried all sorts of approaches at the diplomatic level to regain his conjugal rights : happily without success.

I had a contingent from a bedouin tribe with a long history of desert piracy behind it, the Beni Qitab. One in particular was a huge man with black grapes for eyes and two rows of white teeth shining like a woodman's windows from a thick forest of black beard. He, I thought, might very easily revert to type, as I eyed him in the ranks. And there was a beardless youth with rabbit teeth and eyes like onions who looked as if he would bolt at the sound of his own name. He happened to be the son of the paramount chief of the tribe, a fact to which I allotted insufficient notice at the time.

Such were the characters I took to Tarif. Tarif was a low flat hill rising solitarily from the plain white wilderness of the coast west of Abu Dhabi, about two hundred miles from Sharjah. There is a peak marked on the maps along this coastline, called in Arabic the "High Mountain". It is three hundred feet high. This gives the best possible picture of just how dreary these salt-flats are, and just how many miles of them stretch westwards from Sharjah to Qatar—the whole length of the rhinoceros's brow.

On top of this plateau, which was about sixty feet high and commanded a view of perhaps fifty miles on clear days, was the headquarters of the oil company—an off-shoot of the Iraq

Petroleum Company—which in those days was prospecting for the stuff that is now transforming the pitiful huddle of huts called Abu Dhabi into a new Kuwait. They lived in a village of pre-fabricated air-conditioned buildings and distilled their water (there being none for hundreds of miles in any direction) from the sea. They were an odd crew, these Oily Boys, as we called them to their disgust : tough-talking Texans; even tougher-talking Glaswegians pretending to be Texans; young bespectacled scientists from Birmingham who drank only lime juice, and jolly bearded men who subsisted on nothing but brandy. My most spectacular gastronomical adventures in all Arabia derived from these hospitable people. Once, during my first year, I visited for some reason one of their more far-flung outposts which had camped inland on a dried-up salt lake. There I found a little collection of caravans and tents surrounded on all sides by a vast wilderness of flaming red sand dunes. I arrived in time for lunch.

There were lobsters. There was a choice of fillet steak or roast turkey. And there were strawberries and cream. All, including the strawberries, were fresh—the only food in that camp to come out of a tin was the beer.

So our New Years Eve party at Tarif was not quite the shock to my system it might otherwise have been, here in the depths of the most desolate country on earth. The whole Scotch salmon, the dressed crab, the cold roast duck . . . by a whim of our Colonel's, I was not supposed to share this Babylonian life except by invitation. I myself lived two hundred yards away in a sort of card-house of palm-leaf matting which looked from the out-side like a hurricane-blasted haystack; inside it was like living in a house of breakfast cereal. If it had offered any resistance at all to the winds which swept across those dead-flat steppes it would long ago have scattered its unbeautiful self over half the Empty Quarter; and when it rained the only thing I could do was to erect my spare camp bed, suspend it by the four corners over the one I was sleeping in, and listen to the water pouring off its foot down past my own feet to make a morass of my floor.

Over that first New Year in the wilderness we were cut off entirely by rain. The whole distance to H.Q. in Sharjah was turned into one lake of brine, with here and there the tops of prominent features like Tarif and the High Mountain looming out of the slush. The Oil Company's airstrip took on the consistency of porridge; here and there along the waterlogged road to their jetty were half-sunken lorries dimly seen through the mists like drowned dinosaurs. If I had not had the Oily Boys next door I would have been on short commons, as my baked beans and corned beef (on which I fed myself when not a guest of those epicures) were not everlasting.

But one lonely night we saw a light, far away across the wastes; and it was moving—distinctly approaching—slowly but certainly. It eventually became a Land-Rover, and behind the wheel was Bob Warner our administrative officer—bearing letters, and pay for the troops, and similar comforts. This was about my first meeting with that white-haired unstoppable man, although not my last. I learnt that he had made the journey from Sharjah by keeping his wheels in the wettest part of the marshes; for these were where the salt was compacted by traffic; he had driven two hundred miles through a salt water quagmire, and most welcome he was.

I seem to be preoccupied with transport troubles, but they were indeed our major preoccupation. The operational task of the company at Tarif was to guard the western approaches in case the dreaded Turki should try another incursion; but Turki was the least of our worries on the spot, however much blood the Political Agent may have sweated over him. True, whenever we saw lights to the south of us—in the sands—we had a moment's heart-thumping, until the Oily Boys assured us it was only one of their survey parties marking trigonometrical points with empty whisky bottles as they mapped their merry way over the trackless seas of sand. But otherwise it was the endless warfare between our vehicles and the countryside which dominated life.

One day I was returning from a patrol to the west—where there was nothing except more and more of the same for another four or five degrees of longitude—and as I breasted the slope to our camp I saw what looked like a couple of wallowing whales some hundreds of yards out to sea. It was, as I soon discovered, one third of my transport fleet. The sea-shore at Tarif slopes gently down from high-tide mark, and seems firm; as the only other water is the Oil Company's expensive distillate, the drivers were in the habit of driving down to the beach at high tide and washing their vehicles in the sea. As the tide went out, I was told sadly, the drivers followed its retreat, instead of facing the labour of carrying water further and further up the beach; until, at just about full low tide, there was a simultaneous squelching sound and both monsters broke through the crust and settled comfortably on their axles. Of course, being dutiful soldiers they had waited to report to their commander before doing anything . . . it was now nearly high tide, and the water was lapping over the bonnets. There was nothing to be done until the sea went out again.

As soon as the retreating tide cleared the drowned hulks we all trooped down bearing strips of the steel track which the Oil Company used for making roads and airstrips, and laid a pathway over which one of my precious remaining trucks made its way gingerly towards the two stranded truants, which by this time were glistening with salt and festooned with green weed like exposed wrecks. We just managed to get one out before the incoming tide washed too high about our knees and the axles of the rescue truck; the other one had to wait for another low tide, which this time was in the middle of the night—my Oily friends were regaled to a sort of marine torchlight tattoo, and they cheered from the foreshore. But we saved our trucks from a permanent grave, and Epstein spent many happy hours next day making love to the two salt-caked lorries and warming them back to life with the magic of his touch. . . .

A similar fate overtook a couple of trucks on the way to Abu Dhabi. In those days the only road went across a sort of quicksand. The whole distance was a graveyard of camels, in all stages of decay from still-stinking carcasses to gleaming bones; for if one of the beasts, tied in a caravan, put a foot off the beaten pathway on to the shifting jelly at the side, its leg went in up to the knee and snapped. This journey was only attempted by motor transport in the utmost necessity and with the greatest care. Driving along one could feel the insubstantial surface

34

quivering glutinously underneath, and to stop meant certain disaster.

I forget exactly how or why one of my trucks got itself stuck in this gluttonous bog; the one I took along to haul it out found that its tractive energy, far from pulling its mate out, was merely driving itself in; so there they were, two hulks lolling awkwardly like swamp-bound elephants. The established routine in a case like this is to get out the jack, set it up under the axle, rest it on a hard base—such as a thick board, if you have one handy—and raise the thing until a piece of metal track can be coaxed under the sunken wheel. This we tried. We found a six-inch thick piece of wood which some previous victim had used and left behind as a comfort to travellers, and jacked away. It was soon apparent that our hydraulic lift was having the effect, not of raising the wheel we were working on out of the ooze, but of forcing the opposite one further in—the suction of the stuff was too much for a five-ton jack. When we got down to trying to dig, we could see why. The substance just under the surface was a white paste the colour and consistency of zink oxide; it was an effort to withdraw the hand from a tentative probe, let alone the wheel and axle of a three-ton truck.

Luckily, here we could leave them without danger. They had sunk as far as they could, now resting on their floorboards, and there was no tide to damage them further. A despairing signal to Sharjah brought a sharp reprimand and the M.T. Sergeant with an enormous garage trolley-jack which was powerful enough to prise the lorries out, with a sucking sound.

Not only Epstein was kept busy at Tarif. Gunpowder Joe tied up toes, which were used to the soft sands of Buraimi and got stubbed on the crystallized salt of Tarif—another shattered illusion of mine was the toughness of an Arab's feet; he spooned out doses for my suffering sons of the desert who found that the wintry sea air affected their delicate constitutions. There is nothing, but nothing, more miserable and pathetic than a sick Arab. He sits huddled in a blanket with a blue-green face and tragic eyes and croaks in a sepulchral whisper that he is unable to move. There was never anything more wrong with them than

35

a common cold or chill, or occasional constipation which Gunpowder Joe cured with a spectacular aplomb worthy of his name; but to see the morning sick parade would melt the heart of a Patton. To be fair, there is no man more hardy or long-suffering in the face of physical injury—he can bear a broken bone which would prostrate us; but a touch of flu transforms him into an El Greco martyr. It was lucky that I had Gunpowder Joe with me for most of the time, as when I was alone I was overcome with pity for the pathetic creatures and gave them all leave to stay in bed. But not Joe. With all the authority of a lance-corporal's stripe he forced them out on parade, where they lined themselves up and greeted my inspection with reproachful Belsen-eyes.

These were men who had been in our army for about two months, prior to which they had probably not even seen a European let alone had any contact with European ways of doing things. Their unfamiliarity with our ideas of soldiering has been described. The period of recruit training had been safely under-gone; but the wrinkles were not yet ironed out. One day I was faced with a mutiny. Two hundred miles from Sharjah, with the Oily Boys and their luxurious camp in my care, my company went on strike.

It happened like this. Contrary, yet again, to popular ideas, the Arab as nature made him is not physically strong. He is lean and long-suffering (except when sick), but my soldiers found the ordinary service rifle rather too heavy for them to handle with that slickness and ease which the sergeant major likes to see. So I instituted a loathesome form of P.T. known in the British Army as "rifle strengthening exercises". The object of these is to toughen the wrists and arms of the weedy by having them whirl their rifle around the head, hold it out at arm's length and twist it about, and eventually grasp it by the extreme tip of the muzzle and lift it with a straight arm horizontal from the body.

It was my misfortune that the weediest man of my company was the rabbit-toothed son of the paramount chief of the tribe of Qitab. Almost as inadept at rifle strengthening exercises, despite his ferocious black-bearded aspect, was the other leader of the contingent. They decided after one or two parades that the whole thing was "Shame"; they were being shown up before their fellow-tribesmen and other Arabs as demonstrably feeble, which entailed an intolerable loss of face.

"Shame" is dear to the heart of the Arab in his pristine state. In its nobler application it is the code of chivalry which keeps life in the desert on a level of decency which never prevailed in our own European Age of Chivalry, and in its pettier forms it inhibits a soldier from demonstrating to his M.O. the symptoms of V.D. for which he is requesting a cure. In this particular case, it was "Shame" and unbearably so—that two such illustrious scions of the House of Qitab should be made to perform, in public, gymnastic evolutions which were beyond their powers.

One morning, therefore, as I went out of my haystack-house to survey the parade, I was confronted with first one, then another, and then the whole lot of them, drawing their rifles from the armoury for exercises, laying them down neatly in a pile in the middle of the parade ground, and standing around sheepishly wondering what I—and indeed they—were going to do next.

This, I knew, was the crisis in the development of these men into soldiers. Ridiculous though the incident itself was, and innocent of really mutinous intent though the men were, it was necessary to show who was boss—even though at the time it was fairly apparent that the Beni Qitab chieflings, and not I, were in effective command.

The Trucial Oman Levies were in a peculiar position. Although all their officers—by this time—were serving officers of the British Army, and the force was paid and supplied by the Foreign Office, the men owed no allegiance at all to the British Crown—unlike, for example, Gurkhas or Colonial troops. They owed no allegiance to anybody—they took no oath; so their legal position was obscure and the legal foundation for my authority over them was not of the firmest. There was in being a document setting out the rules and regulations of the force, and expressing disapproval, for example, of "conduct to the prejudice of good order and military discipline"; but it is most unlikely that any of the soldiers had much idea of its existence, let alone significance. On the whole the relationship between officer and man was a personal one, and when that broke down there was little left. One very gallant officer so incensed his men by thoughtless treatment that they turned on him with their bayonets; he was swiftly put on an aircraft for home, and thereafter his men were as good as gold.

So, piffling though my mutiny was, it had a significance which can almost be called historic. It marked the parting of the ways. To these clannish tribesmen, so recently snatched from their camels and dressed up in military khaki—who was to be boss? Their own chiefs, or the infidel with the stars on his shoulder? The entire structure of our enterprise could hinge on these paltry rifle exercises. All through an anxious morning the two sides confronted each other, sullen Arabs armed with a hundredfold majority, apprehensive authority armed only with vague and unenforceable sanctions. In the event, the resolve of the mutineers faltered before mine did : faced with the choice of submission to discipline or irrevocable outlawry, they dropped their eyes one by one; the next two lessons of R.S.E. were taken by myself personally (the reason for this was my own unimpressive physique, which was manifestly unlikely to set them too unrealistic a standard); and the crisis passed. My report of the incident brought the colonel post-haste to investigate the rot, but finding no rot he departed.

Life at Tarif continued its even tenor punctuated by occasional alarms that the fiendish Turki was on his way—who always turned out to be a bibulously erratic Oily Boy—and occasional operations to rescue a lorry from the greedy quagmires.

At last our tour of duty at Tarif was completed, and we set off for home : a convoy of lorries, most of which had been salvaged from the sea at one time or another. There were my chastened mutineers, there was Epstein, Gunpowder Joe; and the whole cavalcade was led by myself in a veteran Land-Rover, bereft of silencer, shock absorbers, and brake shoes, lurching and eructating over the corrugated road to civilization. A spell of refitting lay ahead of us, in Sharjah, and then we were despatched south, over the sand barrier, to the edge of the Forbidden Zone of Buraimi. At Tarif I had had the Oily Boys and their extravagant cuisine for neighbours. At Mahadha, so I learnt, I would be by myself, apart from my soldiers and one or two local inhabitants, and I would have to eat what I could get. Moreover, if I wanted to talk, I would have to talk Arabic, or else hold my peace : this, my elders told me gleefully, would put a fine edge on my fluency in that tongue.

I was still young enough to regard the prospect with enthusiasm.

4

THE FORBIDDEN ZONE

Two prehensile hairy yellow legs groped out from a crevice in the wall. They waved, as if testing the air; then followed a beak like an octopus's; then, helping each other through, the rest of its legs heaved out into the daylight, one by one. The beast was at least eight inches long. If I had been alone I would have forsworn alcohol from that day on.

This was, however, merely my first acquaintance with the hideous spiders of Arabia. The fact that I made it on my very first morning in Mahadha filled me with little love for the place. These spiders have, in addition to their fair share of legs, two long arms which wave around in front of the head. They are a sickly yellow colour, and hairy; not bushy like a bird-eater but more like a gooseberry. The abdomen is fat, as pale and as fleshy as a raw sausage. The mouth is a carnivorous beak, opening into four mandibles; and along the back is a hard carapace. It hunts by rearing up on its hind legs and grabbing flying insects with its arms. It catches a scuttling scorpion in the same way, and as the poisonous tail beats and beats ineffectively against the armour of the spider's back the four jaws are steadily munching their way from front to rear through the captive creature's flesh.

At night the ground was alive with these outsized arachnids, scampering about like rats after a low-flying cricket or prowling stealthily, arms waving hungrily about their heads. One of a family of kittens who shared my palm-leaf hut at Mahadha had a fight with one, which I witnessed. The kitten, about two months old, won; but the spider put up a fight that lasted fully ten minutes.

Spiders lived in the cracks of my house; scorpions were to be expected in, under or between anything they could penetrate. The cats would never go for a scorpion—instinct told them that they were poison, which to give them their due the spiders were not.

Mahadha even had aggressive fish, although it was eighty miles from the sea. The village was watered by a conduit which tapped a water-table in the foothills. Every day in the early afternoon I used to go to a place where the channel was exposed, partly to wash but mainly to get some relief from the roasting heat. The channel was alive with tiny fish, no more than an inch and a half long, which arrived in clouds like miniature piranhas as soon as my body broke the surface. They were too small to do any actual harm but if there was a scratch or any broken skin they went for it and gnawed; and like the Sharjah coral-flies they delighted in the more intimate parts of the body. Grim-faced I sat there until the things drove me mad and I had to leave the deliciously cool water for the oven of my hut. Where these tormenting creatures came from I have never heard adequately explained; the channels draw their water from underground springs, and peter out into the desert when they have passed through the village they serve. You are as likely to find monkeys on a desert island or birds in a pyramid. How did they get there? All I know is they had a taste for my flesh.

Our camp at Mahadha was a neat cantonment of palm-mat huts set among thorn trees in a sandy bowl in the mountains. It was so hot at noon that metal objects inside the house were too hot to grasp; water almost too hot to drink. My cats spent all day curled round an earthenware water-pot on the floor, motionless, tongues lolling, except when I lay bare on the bed when they would come and try to lick me for salt. Here at least we were spared the steam-bath of the coast, and the nights, if not cool, were at least some relief; but from mid-morning until sunset the whole ring of hills around us shimmered steadily as if seen through rippling water, and not so much as an ant stirred.

41

I had left Epstein and Gunpowder Joe behind, and now was my own mechanic and doctor. Thanks to Joe, who had taught the men not to pity themselves, to the summer which had dried up their chills, and to the sand which was kinder to their toes, I had not too much to do; my worst casualty was a corporal with a compound fracture of his little toe, which I poked back into place and tied up with a stub of pencil for a splint.

My medical practice brought me for the first time face to face with a phenomenon I was to meet quite often in the years to come. I was aroused one night from my fly-blown bed by an agitated N.C.O. who reported that one of his soldiers had become possessed of a devil. Cursing soldiers and devils indiscriminately I stumbled out into the hot darkness and across to a barrack hut whence issued screams and gurgles which were entirely unhuman : they were not even recognizably animal. Accompanying this diabolical solo was a chorus of soothing chants. By now scared stiff, but propelled by the N.C.O., I poked my head gingerly inside, and saw a scene straight from Dante. Dimly lit by a guttering lamp in the otherwise pitch-black chamber was a ring of pale intense faces, eyes wide as saucers, swaying rhythmically back and forth and liturgically humming around a struggling body on the floor. Squatting astride the victim were two of the heavier soldiers, whose bulk restrained him from indulging in too violent convulsions. Out of the mouth of this afflicted apparition came the sounds of pandemonium itself. This was clearly no place for me, with my bottles of aspirin and Epsom salts. I withdrew, feeling uneasily in need of personal exorcism, and kept strictly out of the way. I saw the man next morning, on parade, and he seemed in the best of health; I was assured that his temporary guest had departed during the night and returned to the nether regions. I said how glad I was, and the incident passed.

My worst transport casualty came on our way to take over the garrison, while we were traversing the sand barrier—an all-night journey, for some four or five miles. A very new driver came up to us as we were man-handling a truck up a sand-slope and said that his vehicle wouldn't go. We asked him what seemed to be wrong; almost in tears he held up a bone-dry dipstick and said, "There is something the matter with this".

So there, in the midst of the red downs of sand, was a brand-new lorry with an engine seized solid; its cylinders, starved of oil, had fused into one single lump of lifeless iron. There was only one thing to do, and with little hesitation we did it. We removed everything removeable from the wretched truck, and left its husk in the sands, where it still is—although it has no doubt long ago been buried under the shifting dunes.

We had as motor transport officer in those days a mustachioed young man of astonishing ingenuity who had, in fact, on at least one occasion performed the incredible feat of changing an engine in the middle of the sand barrier; but the problem here was too intractable even for him; there were no more engines to be had in the whole of the Trucial States. Our drivers seemed to go through engines as others consume tyres or fan-belts, and none could be expected before the wreck would have been decayed and pillaged beyond hope. It was no more possible to tow a truck over those dunes than over the English Channel.

So we left it; Epstein himself could have done no more.

En route through Sharjah we had picked up another squad of recruits as reinforcements. One of these was an elderly man with kindly eyes who always called me "my son"—and tended to treat me rather more paternally than a company commander expects from his latest recruit. However, I was by now getting used to the eccentricities of the service. In the early days I was astonished, when leading a convoy, finding that all the vehicles behind me had stopped and retracing my steps in wrathful inquiry—to discover the entire complement saying their prayers. Prayers punctuated the day and the whole military programme had to be arranged around them if one was not to find, for example, guard-mounting parade interrupted by sudden but well-drilled obeisances. Another most trying aspect of the Arab character, from a military point of view, was the complete and utter timelessness of their lives. It was impracticable to announce a parade for precisely half past seven: even when the time was translated into Arabic, in which the day starts at sunset (so that "eight o'clock tonight" in our language is "two o'clock tomorrow" in theirs), the prospects for even an approximate response were dim. It was not unusual to find a parade scheduled to last half an hour going on and on interminably until brought to a close by our own desperate intervention.

This Bohemian trait was most marked when soldiers went home on leave. If the timing of a half-hour's drill was likely to vary by one hundred per cent, so too—with far more upsetting results for the company's administration—was a fortnight's home leave. I would instruct the men to begin their leave like an umpire counting the over at cricket, with a pocket or a bag full of fourteen stones, one of which was to be discarded each day; but even this scheme was a prey to human fallibility, especially when the soldier had a hole in his pocket . . . on the whole they took no advantage of this: they were just as likely to return three days early as three days late, and there was a general averaging-out over a period.

My neighbour at Mahadha was the representative of the Sultan dispossessed from Buraimi. His real name was Sayid Salem bin Humaid al Saidi, but we all called him Grock, in respectful memory of that great clown, because he brought joy and delight to our otherwise frustrated and sun-baked lives. He was a born comedian, albeit unwitting.

He inhabited a hairy palm-frond hut about fifty yards from mine, where he was supposed to act as a civilian customs post, auxiliary to my military check-point on the edge of the Forbidden Zone of Buraimi. There was a certain amount of mercantile lorry traffic from the coast to the oasis which, after my sentries had searched it for arms and ammunition and subversive literature, was passed on to Grock to pillage on behalf of the Sultan.

A great deal of mystery surrounds Grock's interpretation of his master's orders and his translation of them into action. I will merely say, objectively, that his hut was an extraordinary lumber-room of assorted comforts which for the most part seemed to have been confiscated from passing trucks. Money, certainly, he never took, except in the shape of customs dues; and he always justified his depredations by a punctilious reference to his orders.

I had many occasions to remonstrate with him, following up

official complaints. With an elfin chuckle and a champing of his empty gums he would then scrabble in a pile of documents on the floor. Out came reams of unreadable Arabic, and Grock, eyes sparkling, recited in a rapid goat-bleat what he claimed were his authority and commission. We both knew what his orders were, but to clarify a point through the smokescreen of incomprehensibility which Grock laid over the debate was beyond my powers.

Grock had no teeth. Luckily, his gummy meeh-ing was always accompanied by a whole repertoire of hand gestures of great scope and lucidity, like a deaf and dumb language. The word "money", for example, or anything pertaining to finance, was illustrated by the thumb and forefinger of the right hand counting imaginary coins to the left. Riding, or travelling, or indefinite camels, was two fingers of one hand astride the forefinger of the other, which then bobbed along like a dromedary. For motor transport he grasped and joggled a tiny imaginary steering wheel. The old fellow had a whole dictionary of these signs, and I could almost carry on a conversation without trying to listen at all.

Surprisingly, he had a dormant but ferocious temper; when the sleeping monster was aroused he became a most formidable old man. He grew, both upwards and outwards; the mild and humorous eyes flashed like a Tartar chief; the gentle old face became that of Jehovah in wrath, the goat-bleat burgeoned into a bull's roar. Luckily the phenomenon took place so seldom that it was an interesting event, like an earthquake, and was quickly dispelled by his chuckles.

With his erratically folded turban of Kashmir shawl, which he would disconcertingly remove—it came off complete, like a made-up hat, revealing a pumpkin-bald pate which he then scratched; with his dignified robes and ceremonial dagger, to which the twinkling eyes and toothless chuckles gave an air of fancy dress; with his floor littered with documents, letters, petitions, of which the one he wanted was always somewhere else so that he crawled about on all fours like a bear, rummaging; Grock was one of the most delightful men I knew. He gave me an opportunity, too, of getting my own back for all the goat-crowned mounds of rice that I was by now regarding with increasing biliousness the more I saw—I used to invite Grock over for dinner, and rend great hunks of flesh into chunks with gusto and pile the pieces up in front of him until he choked . . . he used to belch most handsomely.

At Mahadha, too, I made the acquaintance of another grand old man of Oman. He first came into my life out of a brassy sky, shortly before the end of my posting, in response to a rumour in Sharjah that I was going out of my mind. He came swooping down in one of those old flying green-houses, the Avro Anson, to see for himself. The Anson scudded to a halt, momentarily disappearing in its own dust, and out he climbed. A great black up-curving moustache, apple cheeks, and a filthy blue cap introduced themselves. "Jasper," he said.

Everybody called him Jasper. It was certainly not his real name—his initial was K, although nobody knew what it stood for. But "Jasper" in that part of the world had long ceased to bring to mind a villain of Victorian melodrama; it was inseparable from a large and kindly group captain with a reputation for eccentricity.

More intriguing than his moustache or even his name was an oblong wooden box, cunningly made of some exotic timber, slung over his shoulder; it bounced as he strode along with his huge shillelagh of a walking stick. He enlightened me, kindly. It was, he said, a camera box; a camel camera box; it was made of Bo wood.

Jasper only stayed a short while—long enough to satisfy himself that reports of my mental unhingement were, as the saying goes, greatly exaggerated (I had implied, as far as I remember, in a telegram to H.Q. that if something or other did not happen I would have no recourse but to shoot myself—which report, taken at face value by an over-literal duty officer, had brought this visitation by the group captain).

I was to see a great deal more of both Jasper and Grock in the years to come.

Mysterious manœuvres were taking place in the unknown territory to the south of us. In those days Oman Proper, the

Green Mountains, the domain of the Imam, was a legendary land redolent of romance. There, it was said, the dry and forsaken wastes of sand gave way to green-clad hills, sparkling streams, castellated cities with bannered turrets and spice-rich markets; mountains soared to the clouds and beyond, carpeted with misty meadows, where grapes and pomegranates, walnuts and nectarines dropped ripe into the outstretched hand . . . there reigned the Imam, cloaked in mystic splendour, and there stalked Suleiman bin Himyar, Lord of the Green Mountains, King of Nebhania, unchallenged tyrant of the verdant plateau . . . this was the image we had of those regions, delineated on our maps with only the scantiest of detail. One explorer had, in recent years, skirted the inhabited districts but had never penetrated the hills.

However, odd things had been happening, in the utmost secrecy—so secret that although I, at Mahadha, was supposed to be playing the part of a sort of long-stop to the operation, nobody told me at the time. A peculiar band known as the Muscat and Oman Field Force had established themselves at a town called Ibri, some hundred miles to the south of Buraimi and half-way house to Oman Proper. Since they had not passed through Buraimi we assumed that they had made their way there from the opposite direction, up from the deep south across the desert. My first inkling of this egregious army was an instruction that I was to escort a convoy of civilian lorries through Mahadha on its way from Sharjah to Ibri—a formidable journey—bearing petrol for the Field Force. They had completely out-run their own line of communications and this was the only way they could keep themselves on the road.

So one morning, before sunrise, I took a small patrol to the Mahadha side of the sand barrier, to await their coming. All this was done in the most deep and confidential obscurity. I was to ensure that under no circumstances was the convoy to set foot over the boundary of the Buraimi zone. I was to hand the convoy over, at a certain small and secret hill, to representatives of the Muscat and Oman Field Force who would rendezvous at the suitable hour of midnight and spirit it away into the depths of the Arabian peninsula.

All went as planned. A low grumbling, as of distant thunder, rolled sullenly over from the other side of the sand barrier; it was the sound of many vehicles churning and grinding their way up and over the dunes. Some hours later the first truck arrived. By midday the last of them had come waddling down the slippery red slopes of sand, on pillow-flat tyres. Ranging from ten-ton leviathans to little wooden-bodied pick-ups, each bore a full stack of 44-gallon drums. It was now, being full day, far too hot for anything else to happen until the sun had begun to bend to the west. When at last it began to cool, each truck disgorged a small half-naked black boy with a pump as tall as himself, and the next couple of hours were beguiled by the pumping up of tyres: small boys bobbed rhythmically over their machines, while in the shade of the thorn trees could be seen the gently-heaving bellies of the resting drivers.

At last, towards evening, the convoy was ready. I and my patrol had been there since early morning, making sure the sacred borders of the Buraimi zone were not violated. When all the tyres had been blown up, and all the drivers had awoken and made and drunk their pots of tea, we set off towards Mahadha twenty-five miles further on. There the fleet was marshalled— which is to say it milled and ground around the camp, lowing like a herd of cows, refusing under any circumstances to do what it was told; while I prepared myself for the meeting with the ambassadors from Ibri.

We managed, by persuasion and threats, to keep the convoy the right side of the boundary, and after dark I took off for the rendezvous. This had been carefully pinpointed as a pinnacle of rock in the middle of a wide depression in the hills to the south of us. On the map, it was a perfectly clear and unmistakable meeting-point: there was the valley, and there, neatly delineated in mauve ink, was a distinct and isolated knoll. It was only as I approached the area that the deficiencies of the Military Survey in that part of the world became apparent. The whole floor of the valley was an eruption, a positive acne of knolls.

I drove disconsolate from hill to hill, calling up to each with growing despair; when suddenly the night was illuminated by a shower of pistol-flares.

An unmistakable rattle of loading musketry and the sinister murmur of urgent nocturnal commands raised the pimples of my skin—and a crisp voice, in the clearest, most crystal-limpid English, sliced down from one of the innumerable rocks:

"Halt."

We stamped hard on the anchors, showering ourselves with dust in the rising moonlight.

"Declare yourselves," said the well-modulated voice.

Only the happy coincidence that I, too, spoke English saved the incident from ending bloodily. I was able to reply: "Trucial Oman Levies," in at least as well-cultured tones as my challenger.

"Dismount and be identified."

Out I got, and stood—trembling—with outstretched arms while a couple of khaki-clad soldiers slithered down the knoll and shone torches in my face, examining me minutely.

They shouted reassuring words up to the peak, and shortly two British officers descended and joined us. They, too, satisfied themselves that I was not Turki in disguise, and together we drove back to Mahadha where the convoy of petrol-lorries was handed over to them—to my huge relief. For some hours afterwards I could hear the mingled expostulations of my cultured friends from Ibri, the disgruntled grumblings of the Sharjah truckers, and the crescendo concert of lorries starting up. I fell asleep then; when I awoke in the morning, they had all gone, leaving only a deep trail of ruts which led into the depths of central Arabia.

A little while after this, my eighteen months with the Trucial Oman Levies came to an end. I bade farewell to Grock, and to the grizzled soldier who called me his son; stepped carefully over my last obscene yellow spider; handed over my men and my commission to an excellent man named John Rhodes, and took off for Sharjah and the sodden skies of London.

I was to miss the most stirring events in Buraimi, and the most historic developments in Oman Proper. For the next two years I strove with little success to be, first, regimental signals officer of my battalion in Germany, and secondly a Royal Air Force pilot.

Meanwhile, the twentieth century burst rudely upon the slumber of centuries in the Sultanate of Muscat and Oman.

5

SULTAN VERSUS IMAM

THE patient negotiations in Geneva collapsed when the diplomatic methods of the Saudi Arabian delegation became too blatant to be ignored any further. To be brief, they made up for their lack of cogent legal argument by a liberal distribution of cash; which, while a perfectly normal and acceptable practice in their own traditions, came as something of a shock to the smooth lounge-suited men on the other side of the table.

The result of this was that the Trucial Oman Levies were unleashed. The coup de main that the Sultan had been forbidden to carry out in 1952, was delivered at the end of 1955.

It was stirring stuff. Under the crisply capable leadership of Eric Johnson, who brought his striking force to Mahadha in the guise of a relieving company, the Levies swooped down on the Saudi police at break of day and rounded them up before they could put their trousers on. On the way they had seized the person of the man who was to be installed as Sultan's representative in Grock's old magistracy. He, however, was not allowed to know. He was to all intents and purposes kidnapped, and held incommunicado, until the bewildered fellow was borne into Buraimi and dumped into his palace.

The Levies re-occupied the oasis in force, choosing for their garrison a broken-down castle of peculiar shape—it looked more like a castle-pudding than anything else—which they rebuilt; and as a sop to the Sultan a detachment of his army was invited to establish itself in Buraimi fort.

50

And that, so everybody thought at the time, was that.

But the delay had been disastrous. The years between that descent of the dusty Consul General on the Sultan's tribal horde, and the ultimate ejection of the Saudi police detachment from the oasis, had been used too well by the wily proconsuls of the King. Buraimi and the Trucial States were—at least to the unaided eye—free from infection, healthily healing after the operation. But the disease had spread, and to the south, in the cool palm-filled valleys and antique cities of Oman itself, Saudi moneybags had found greedy hands.

For almost all of its recorded history—which covers over two thousand years—Oman had been independent, turning its back on the rest of Arabia and the world. For a short while it was ruled bloodily by the Caliphs of Baghdad; but apart from isolated epochs, dimly seen in the tapestry of its story, Oman ruled itself in its own peculiar way. At times there were kings—the Nebhan dynasty, Lords of the Green Mountain and ancestors of the present Lord, Suleiman bin Himyar, who still called himself King of Nebhania when nobody was looking. Sometimes there was an Imam; sometimes, indeed, there were two Imams, and there were periods also when there was no Imam at all nor any recognizable authority.

The eighteenth century was a time of two Imams, who kept up a sporadic civil war until one of them engaged a mercenary soldier named Ahmed bin Said to exterminate the other. In due course, in true Roman fashion, Ahmed bin Said himself became Imam. The Imamate was not supposed to be hereditary, but Ahmed's family soon made it so. Nor was it supposed to rule from Muscat, the coastal town where there were infamous contacts with Christians and other defiling elements, but from Nizwa, the most secret and holy of all the cities in the bowels of Oman. Ahmed's dynasty soon altered that however, and they set themselves up as Imams of Muscat and Oman. It was not long before they committed another infamy and appropriated to themselves the alien title of Sultan. This was altogether too much for the scented hierarchs of the interior, who riposted by electing their own Imam from among their more pious chieftains.

51

Thus there arose the situation, which obtained off and on for some century and a half, of an Imam of Oman and a Sultan of Muscat and Oman. There were many complex variations; sometimes the Sultan called himself Imam, for a while; there was the occasional interregnum when there was no Imam in the interior. There were periods when the Sultan and Imam co-existed in the greatest harmony, the Sultan recognized as titular overlord but the Imam virtually autonomous in the interior.

Such a situation obtained in the early 1950s. The Imam was wise, respected, and just, and the Sultan and he were on the whole on the best of terms. When the Sultan reacted to Turki's blitzkrieg by summoning the tribes to eject him, it was the Imam who provided the greater part and the most warlike of the warriors. He was a rigid opponent of outside influence, Christian, pagan, or Saudi, and wanted no foothold of the King within the frontiers of Oman.

Unfortunately he died, soon after the events recorded in the first chapter of this chronicle. Powerful interests set to work on the selection of his successor. Turki's money, despite the vigilance of the Levies, had penetrated to the inmost depths of Oman; and the man who finally bubbled up to the surface of the Imamate in April 1954 was, to all intents and purposes, a Saudi puppet. His name was Ghalib bin Ali. He had a brother, whose name of Talib would be—like Danton's in the French Revolution—"tolerably well known" in the years which were to follow.

Backing Ghalib for his own purposes was Suleiman bin Himyar, from the top of his craggy kingdom; also backing him from the distant province of Sharqiya further south was a local potentate called Saleh bin Issa. With Suleiman and his mountain, Saleh and his province, and his own powerful tribe as well, the new Imam had a formidable grip on the country inland of Muscat.

Enter an oil company. Another off-shoot of the Iraq Petroleum Company had long nourished an interest in the desert fringes of Oman, attracted by a conspicuous dome of rock called Fahud which so resembled their text-book illustrations of an oil-bearing feature that they found it irresistible. But now there developed a diplomatic and juridical dispute. The Sultan claimed, as nominal overlord of the whole land, that he and he only should treat with the Oily Boys; besides, it was a matter of external policy, which had always been his prerogative.

"Not so," said the Imam and his cabal. "If anything is an internal affair, it is oil; nothing could be more internal than the oil deep in the bosom of our earth".

Faced with this impasse the British Government gave encouragement to the Sultan for a coup de main. The prospect of an oil-field, operated by a British company, with an exit to the ocean outside the vulnerable narrows of the Persian Gulf, was attractive to H.M.G.; and the prospect to the Sultan of laying his hands physically on his fertile hinterland cannot have been without its charm. Hence the peculiar rumours, the backwash which lapped at our feet so far north as Mahadha; hence the secret meeting at the knoll, the intractable petrol convoys, and the rest of the drama. The oil company bespoke a special native army, grandiloquently christened the Muscat and Oman Field Force, to accompany them on a blitzkrieg of their own by which they meant to seize Fahud and dig it up. The Field Force in their unbridled enthusiasm charged north to Ibri and took that town in an intoxicating but bloodless escapade. Finally, as a grand finale to the whole triumph, the Sultan allowed himself to be borne away from his palace through the desert to Nizwa—holy Nizwa—where, temporarily discomfited and anxious to gain time, the Mountain King met him and paid him homage. The Imam abdicated; Suleiman, having made his gesture, stalked back up his mountain again; all seemed to be trumpets and roses and cheering Omanis. Saleh bin Issa slipped quietly out of the country.

One small cloud floated over this happy scene, unnoticed at the time. The Imam's brother Talib was captain of a fortress on the seaward side of the mountains, named Rostaq. At the same time as the Sultan's motorcade was driving for Nizwa, Talib was being besieged by one of the Sultan's three private armies—this one was called the Batina Force—under a rotund and arthritic but wise and placid officer called Colin Maxwell. The news of the Imam's abdication reached Talib too late; he had defied Maxwell and his troops, had been hard pressed; when at last the news came straggling wearily in from its long journey over the hills, Talib was for the high jump. But he scorned to surrender. He crept out of his castle by night, crept through Maxwell's encircling braves, and in fact crept all the way to Saudi Arabia—where he began to work at once for a come-back.

It was not long after the establishment of the Sultan's rule in Nizwa that Talib began to recruit, and, under the benign eye of King Saud, to train, an army of liberation, with which he meant to restore the Imamate to its glory.

Suleiman stayed on his mountain, where nobody could reach him anyway, biding his time and striding from village to village selecting his companion for the night. The tyrant had a stick, which he would place over the lintel of his choice's door. When the good man of the house returned from the day's labour and saw that symbol, he would discreetly keep out of the way until the horrible old reprobate had finished with his wife. Suleiman bin Himyar was a thoroughly nasty old man.

Saleh bin Issa had left on a business trip. Soon enough his business took him to Talib's place of exile. The plot was thickening.

In the meantime the Muscat and Oman Field Force charged about their conquered dominions in Land-Rovers, setting up garrisons, building camps. Slowly, so slowly as to be imperceptible at first, the storm-clouds built up and gathered. Suleiman was infallibly courteous whenever the officers met him—not on his mountain, he never let them up there, but at his capital of Tanuf on the plain at the foot of a colossal cliff; but the rumours multiplied, the people of Talib's country grew surly and secretive, and the situation, in the words of the intelligence reports, deteriorated.

Finally in the summer of 1957 the storm burst.

Talib's original plan had been for a two-pronged rebellion, to erupt simultaneously in Saleh bin Issa's province and in central Oman; Saleh's brother Ibrahim bin Issa was to lead the southern flank, and Talib was to lead the centre. This plan went awry, due to a dhow breaking down. Ibrahim arrived in April, duly tried to rouse the Sharqiya, met, to his disgust, a scanty response from the lethargic populace. The Field Force drove down in their

54

Land-Rovers to confront him. The Field Force and Ibrahim made faces at each other, for a while; then learning of the breakdown of Talib's dhow, Ibrahim travelled to Muscat to talk things over quietly with the Sultan. On arrival he was without ado flung into prison, where he probably still is, and peace was restored to Oman.

It was however a deceptive peace. For Talib had not cancelled his voyage. He got another dhow—or else his first one was repaired; sailed with a few score of armed followers; landed on the coast north of Muscat, which is a densely populated area of many villages and date-groves but where he was apparently undetected; and marched resolutely inland.

The first the Field Force knew of this calamitous turn in events was the news that Talib had arrived in Balad Sait. Balad Sait was his home town and capital, a strongly fortified place in a hill-girt bowl some twenty miles north of Nizwa. There he ran up his standard and proclaimed the restoration of the Imamate. His brother Ghalib had little choice but to acquiesce. He joined Talib from the town where he had been living a well-behaved life as a private citizen, and became Imam again. The banner of revolt had been unfurled.

Suleiman in these days was in Muscat. The Sultan had invited him there, as a wise precautionary measure; but as Suleiman had so far behaved himself quite well he was merely put in house arrest.

The Field Force took up Talib's challenge. They could do little else: the countryside was turning increasingly hostile against them and the Sultan whose rule they represented. They got into their Land-Rovers once more and bucketed off to Balad Sait.

The road to Balad Sait passes through some rocky hills, where the track twists and turns among the boulders like a serpent. Being men of military upbringing, the Field Force regarded their line of communications with an uneasy eye; but all was well, they were assured; a friendly tribe, the Abriyin, who were thought to loathe Talib and his clan, would seize the heights and hold them against ambuscade and sabotage. So the Field Force disembogued on to the dusty bowl, from where they could see the towers and walls of Balad Sait a short way off.

Battle was joined at once. The Field Force shot at the towers with their guns. These were Kipling screw-guns—it was at some point in this stage of the proceedings that the commissariat discovered that the only remaining ammunition for this artillery, anywhere in the world, was in the Imperial War Museum in London, and the old warriors were retired. They also shot at the towers with their mortars, and their machine guns. Talib's men shot back with rifles. In this retaliatory way the battle raged for some seven days and nights.

Down in Muscat Suleiman had sniffed the air and decided which way the wind was blowing. One night he slipped his guards, got into his car, and took off for the hills and the battlefield. On the way he met a Field Force Land-Rover, evacuating wounded from Balad Sait to Muscat; he stopped the Land-Rover, had the wounded men shot, and sent it on its way again with its grizzly load to demoralize the troops in Muscat.

As soon as Suleiman reached the foothills of his own mountain kingdom he declared war. His whole tribe rose for the Imam. This meant that not only his impregnable massif of Jebel Akhdhar but all the towns and villages around its foot, all the way to the northern suburbs of Nizwa, were now in arms against the Field Force, and an Omani village in arms means every able-bodied male wagging his weapon over the garden wall. The Field Force were hopelessly cut off from their base camp the other side of Nizwa. They were trapped, between Talib's gun-proof towers and Suleiman's bristling villages. To make things worse, the Abriyin who were supposed to be guarding that treacherous route through the hills had failed to turn up; the Force's trucks were ambushed and blown up on mines.

Quite clearly there was only one thing to do. They must fight their way out, back to their base. The story of this retreat has never to my knowledge been published. It was frightful; and it was in its way magnificent. The Force numbered two companies, plus artillery and headquarters. The distance was about twenty miles, of mountainous defiles and boulder-strewn tracks and streets winding through villages where every window, every garden wall was alive with Arabs, eyes screwed to their sights and fingers bent on the trigger.

The temperature was about 120 degrees fahrenheit.

Not very many of those who had set off for Balad Sait returned to harbour. At one stage the leading troops were actually elbowing rifles out of their way, so close were they, poking over the wall along a narrow lane. Drivers abandoned their vehicles and made for the hills; their passengers were left to make their way as best they could. In choking peppery dust, in cruel noonday heat and elbow-nudging death, a small contingent fought through. The European officers all made it, one of them only narrowly—he was one who had chosen to go on foot over the hills, and he was saved from death of thirst and sunstroke by his sergeant major who refused to leave him. For the rest, some died in the waterless blistering rocks as they wandered away—anywhere away from the firing; others were taken by Talib.

The shattered remnants lost no time in making off for Fahud and the oil camp, safe across eighty miles of desert; whence they were eventually evacuated to the coast. The garrison of Nizwa castle was abandoned to Talib's mercy.

The white flag of the Imam flew again over Nizwa.

Talib's warriors wandered over the deserted Field Force barracks, poking and pecking like carrion crows, looting what they wanted and shooting holes in what they could find no use for.

Delirious fugitives lay down to die in the sweltering bone-dry hills.

The Sultan sent a request for military aid from Britain.

I had chosen this precise moment to apply for a post with the Sultan's army. I must be quick to add that this was no heroic rallying to any Sultan's plea for help. It was pure coincidence : the news of the disasters in Oman had not made the newspapers when I, being politely requested to abandon my ambitions of piloting Her Majesty's aircraft, had cast around for fresh pastures and remembered that the Sultan of Muscat and Oman recruited mercenaries for his army. One of these I now became. Only as the process of interview and medical ground through its formalities did the daily papers begin to fasten their teeth on the news from Nizwa. By then I was committed, and flew out to Muscat wondering what on earth I had let myself in for.

6

"NOTHING YOU COULD CALL NEWS"

Who is the Sultan of Muscat and Oman?
Is he a yes-man or a no-man?
Is he noblest, like the Roman,
Or abominable like the Snowman?
Is he a pro or anti status-quo man?

THESE verses from *Time* magazine are indicative of what the rest of the world felt about the Sultan when his name first resounded from the international headlines. His Highness Sayid Said bin Taimur bin Feisal bin Turki al Saidi . . . there is an irresistible fascination to being a Sultan, like being Caliph of Baghdad or Akond of Swat; and there is a refulgence about multiple titles, Duke of Medina-Sidonia, Prince of Saxe-Coburg-Gotha, Bishop of Bath and Wells—although the total population of the Sultan's titular domains did not exceed half a million, and those that actually acknowledged his suzerainty versus the Imam were perhaps two hundred thousand, still he bore his bifurcated royalty with a panache that the Tsar of All the Russias might have envied.

I met this splendid man shortly after arrival at Muscat. This was about two weeks after the destruction of the Field Force, and the counter-attack was building up fast—the hope was to get the whole operation over and done with before the wolves of the press began to howl, the lessons of Suez 1956 having been well learnt.

His Highness's forces were mustering in Muscat. These con-

58

sisted of the Muscat Regiment (a largely ceremonial body of men under a trim ex-trooper named Frank Haugh), and detachments from the training depot under a man of terrifying whiskers and extravagant gestures called Pat Gray. Over all was enthroned a colonel of Machiavellian kidney, Pat Waterfield, who gave lustre to the office of Chief of Staff. The soldiers in Muscat were forming up into a column, led by Frank Haugh, and christened Haughcol; their task was to force a passage up the narrow mountain road towards the uplands of inner Oman, as best they could, while the main offensive was launched from Fahud driving in from the desert. Not much was expected of Haughcol, due to the hazardous route it had been allotted—a hundred miles of rocky defiles, deep ravines, and tight palm-choked valleys—altogether as distasteful a way, militarily speaking, as the Khyber Pass. The main hope of the Sultan and the British reposed in the Fahud offensive. The troops for this were the soldiers of the plump but reliable Colin Maxwell, some bloodthirsty Scotsmen from the British Army, and a strong contingent of the Trucial Oman Scouts.

I must explain that in the year and a half since I left them the Trucial Oman Levies had undergone a face-lift. They had changed their uniform, for a start. No longer did their officers swoop around the countryside dressed in whatever they fancied or had left; now they adorned themselves with a flourishing red head-cloth with bobbing tassels, like so many Glubbs Pasha. Nor did they now call themselves Levies. In an effort to recruit what they hoped would be the "right type" of officer, the authorities had rechristened them Trucial Oman Scouts. What the precise psychological significance of this change might be, only an advertising man could say; the new force were no more Scouts than the Levies had been; but to do the planners justice, it was now noticeably richer in what was presumably considered the "right type". And the biggest change was at the top. Eric Johnson had gone, and a ferociously-mustachioed, carnivorous-looking man called Stewart Carter had taken over. I have seen no more romantic figure than Stewart Carter, his head and shoulders wrapped in a flaming red head-scarf, moustaches at the high port, crouched fanatically over the steering-wheel of a stripped-down Land-Rover. I am sure that the time had come for the Trucial Omans to be weaned of Eric Johnson's nursing and to be brought up on the stronger meat of a man like Stewart Carter; and under him they certainly looked more and more military every day. He looked superb himself, too.

Wandering incongruously around among swarthy bearded soldiers and eccentric mercenary officers were one or two pink young men in khaki with blue hats. These were annexed from the Royal Air Force, and they carried portable wireless sets with which they could summon aeroplanes to our aid when required. Here was a colossal advantage. During the days of indecision, between the evacuation of the Field Force and the mustering of these armies of liberation, the Air Force had been busy : flying menacingly over the castles and fortresses of Talib's conquests—dropping leaflets exhorting the tribes to overthrow the usurper, declare their loyalty to His Highness, and so save themselves from the gathering wrath—and even shooting anti-tank rockets into the more obvious of Talib's strongholds, and straffing Suleiman bin Himyar's car. Some confusion was caused during these pre-liminaries, by the fact that the Imam's flag was white, and the Sultan's red. At first the pilots mistook the white standards of the Imamate for symbols of surrender, and the red flags which people fluttered desperately out of their windows whenever they heard the Venoms approaching were taken for bloody banners of defiance . . . the matter was further confounded by a few enthusiasts who unfurled the black flag of Holy War, and although these were the worst and most fanatical of the rebels their black banner was given a wide berth by the bewildered pilots.

The rockets did little damage, we afterwards found, although they must have made an almighty noise in the close-packed towns. Most of the forts were of mud, and the rockets merely made a neat hole straight through; and one of them, the great fort of Nizwa, was of solid rock, like a small mountain itself, and the rockets just went "bang" on the outside and dislodged a few flakes of plaster.

However, we now had the Boys in Blue at our side to give close support to the advancing columns. Until now the pilots had been strictly forbidden to attack living targets; they could only shoot at the forts after a couple of diving dummy-runs to warn the people that the R.A.F. was coming. But now the rules were changed. The blue-capped officers were under military orders and could summon the pilots to shoot wherever so required by the soldiery.

While the main punch was gathering strength out at Fahud, supplied and reinforced from the air, the gallant Haughcol was being drawn up on the parade ground of Bait-al-Falaj. This was the headquarters and barracks of the Muscat garrison, situated about five miles outside Muscat itself in a mountain-girdled plain; a neat white four-square fort with a row of neat white barrack blocks. On a rocky eminence stood the house of Pat Waterfield, clad in bougainvillea, and on another eminence was the slightly smaller house of Frank Haugh bedecked in frangipani. The heat was so intense that we could smell it, like the vapour of hot iron, and the nights were like the nights at Sharjah—steamy and heavy as new-baked bread—and here too, the whisky flowed like water.

Haughcol took shape, busily; Haugh's guardsmen, in little khaki pillbox hats; Gray's recruits, awkward in their alien uniform; gunners, with bright new light artillery in place of the Kipling guns; mortars, machine guns; perhaps a hundred souls. And here we were, the day before launching ourselves into the mile-high mountains and the hazards of war, being reviewed by the Sultan of Muscat and Oman.

He was a small man of immense force. He radiated authority, quietly, without seeming to do anything at all. He was middle aged, of rather negroid features, with a combed and scented white beard worthy of the King of Spain. He wore a brightly-coloured turban with a tassel and a black muslin cloak, gold-edged; a gold-encrusted dagger glistened on his belly. He courteously acknowledged my salute, asking me polite questions in fastidiously perfect English; he floated graciously between the ranks, questioning Arab soldiers in Arabic, Indians in Hindustani. He was really no more than a petty and utterly obsolete tyrant, and he no more

61

commanded my allegiance, except insofar as he paid my wages, than any other employer I might have served—but this small, perfumed, slightly corpulent character from the Arabian Nights called to my mind the dialogue of Lear and the disguised Kent:

"You have that in your countenance which I would fain call master."

"What's that?"

"Authority."

I know that the Sultan inspired the most devoted loyalty in those of his soldiers who met him and to whom he made himself known. When, the next year, he withdrew from Muscat to his private domain of Salala many hundred miles to the south he lost this touch with his men, and the spirit went out of them.

Haughcol took off towards the hills, looming sinister and blue on the horizon eighty miles away. We had been delayed at the last minute because the Indian contractor who was to supply our transport had not got our trucks ready—they were still out on jobs, bringing in fish from up the coast, carting building poles, paraffin tins, and generally trading around. For the Sultan's force at Muscat was a static one, and had no motor fleet of its own; and the mechanized arm had been shattered in the retreat from Balad Sait.

So at last we bucketed and bounced out of Bait-al-Falaj, in ruinous Land-Rovers and wooden-sided fish-lorries, feeling rather like the French Army before Paris in 1914. The greater part of our route lay along a populous valley called Wadi Sumail, where a succession of battlemented towns, turreted hills, walls and watch-towers and thick green date-groves lined a river which wound between the colossal heaving flanks of the Jebel Akhdhar—the Green Mountain—on one side and jagged black lava crags on the other. The people of the Wadi Sumail, we were assured, were loyal—like the Abriyin at Balad Sait? we wondered—but at the head of the valley the track climbed up out of it on to the central plateau of Holy Oman itself, in the dominions of Suleiman bin Himyar, and at the watershed we could expect to be shot at.

On the way we were joined by a horrifying horde of Loyal

Tribesmen. Their task was to take over the villages of Suleiman and Talib as we seized them. It was recognized that our hundred men were scarcely an overwhelming power; but, it was argued by the council of war, with our guns and our aeroplanes we could at least ferret the rabbles of the Imam out, and the Loyal Tribesmen would then sweep in and stop them getting back again.

We met up with this calamitous crowd at our first night-stop in the Wadi Sumail. The Indian contractor was making a fortune out of this war—at least a dozen more of his lorries were lined up at the roadside, each filled to overflowing with a cheering mob of brightly-turbaned men, brandishing firearms of every imaginable sort—we thought, like the Duke of Wellington, that whatever effect they might have on the Imam by God they terrified *us*. So many wild men, armed to the eyebrows, with not so much as a vestige of discipline, were an alarming accompaniment. But at least they were apparently on our side.

In charge of this host was a half-brother of the Sultan, Tariq by name. Tariq was half-Turkish; he had been educated in Germany; he spoke German and English better than he spoke Arabic; he liked Beethoven, played a good hand of bridge and was altogether an incongruous Prince of the Blood in a feudal barony like Muscat. However, such was the rôle his fate had allotted him, and he played it dutifully. He was corpulent but active, of huge dignity and gentle charm. I was to see a lot of Tariq in the years to come and to be grateful for the chance to know him, a cultured gentleman forced into the part of medieval chancellor, and visibly rent between genuine loyalty to his brother the Sultan and a sad recognition of how the world was passing his home-land by.

On the evening of the second day we had left the huzzaing tribesmen behind and reached, without alarm or even excursion, the head of the Wadi Sumail. To our right the Jebel Akhdhar soared impossibly to the sky : great grey slabs rearing a mile straight up out of the valley floor. There were the ramparts and buttresses of Suleiman's stronghold. Every few miles, where the walls were split by a ravine, the top of the table-land could be seen through the gash : a creamy grey colour, misty with distance and altitude, speckled with bushes. The greenness of the Green Mountain was not apparent; if I had been expecting lush meadows and leafy forests clothing its crags, I was disappointed. The Arabic language is poorly endowed with colours, so that a camel, for example, may be described as red, white, or green, where we would differentiate subtle shades of yellow-brown and grey. So with mountains. Oman is full of mountains; there are Red Mountains, Black ones, White ones; all are really just different tones of rock-colour. The Jebel Akhdhar's peculiar shade of slate-grey was seen by the inhabitants as nearer to green than anything else. So much for the emerald grassy downs which so many people believed to rise from the Arabian desert in the secret places of Oman.

We eyed these misty battlements uneasily over our shoulders as we jolted up the valley. It was not so much their height which made them so daunting, though the topmost pinnacle is at ten thousand feet; it was the altogether startling abruptness of their leap up from the floor, the sheer smoothness and steepness of their rise, which made them look like the walls of a titanic fortress rather than mere mountains; that, and the way they march away straight into the distance for thirty miles or so until they abruptly turn off at right-angles, with a peak like a giant corner-tower where they turn.

However, our business was not with the Jebel Akhdhar—yet. At the head of the Wadi Sumail the river curved and vanished into a gorge. Before us the stony track wound up a precipice to vanish over its lip. When we were up there, on the plateau of Oman Proper, we would find no water until we had captured a village. Ahead, perhaps fifty miles away, through and beyond the mountains, were Stewart Carter and his Scouts; Colin Maxwell and his men; the Scots; the lot. But here we felt very small, few and alone.

Expecting any minute a hail of bullets from defenders at the top, we headed our trucks for the slope and charged up. We made it without incident—why Talib had made no effort to hold this back door we never discovered. With a final heave and a cloud of dust we breasted the crest and there we were : in the Courts of the Imam. Ahead of us the mountain stretched away towards Nizwa. The upland plain, studded and crusted with hills of black lava, formidable in themselves but dwarfed to mere pimples by the Jebel Akhdhar, faded into the evening mists. Ten or fifteen miles away, invisible, were the first of Suleiman's towns—Mutti and Izki, I noted from my map—fortified, and presumably bristling with fanatical armed men; each with its rock-mounted castle, battlemented walls draped over the hills, watch-towers perching on pinnacles. Mutti nestled close against the foot of the Jebel itself, even clambering a short way up its skirts; Izki lay out in the open, but beyond a range of black crags through which the road wound twistingly, and which we supposed to be as infested with snipers as a dog with fleas.

But at least we had put our foot in the door. We made camp for the night, with our trucks all round us like a Boer laager. Our precious water supply, being below us in the valley-head, was safely in our hands. We built low stone barricades, in lieu of trenches. We picqueted a couple of lumpy hills on our flanks. The great grey hulk of the mountain seemed ominously close, but there must have been at least two miles to its foot, and no sniper in its crevices could harm us. We were comfortable enough.

Just at dusk we saw a lone figure jogging down the track from the sunset; a little grey-bearded man astride a little grey donkey. We blinked: a messenger from the Imam? A fugitive? An apparition? It turned out to be one Rashid bin Harib, chieftain of part of the Wadi Sumail: a wizened gnome with eyes of impenetrable gloom. He had been visiting friends, he told us. No, he had no news. Oh yes, on being pressed, there was some business of a rebellion; he had heard, so it seemed, that the Sultan's army had been evicted . . . that the Imam was back . . . nothing you could call news. Rashid expressed no interest at all in us or our errand. As he climbed aboard his donkey to resume his journey he tossed out, as casually as one mentioning the time of day: "I met Suleiman bin Himyar at Mutti. He is well. He has six hundred men and says he is going to slaughter you all tonight. God is Great." He bobbed away down the track towards Sumail.

Arabs have their own ideas of what constitutes news. When the Field Force had made its epic dash to Ibri, bearing with it the Sultan's representative, that gentleman paid a courtesy call on the Imam's governor who was until then in power. They sipped coffee, discussed the weather, the price of dates, the condition of grazing; each assured the other that there was no news. Finally, the Sultan's man stood up to take his leave. "Oh by the way," he said, "there is just one thing—the Sultan's army is outside and they are going to bombard the town if you don't clear out within the hour. Good-bye, and thank you so much for the coffee."

We strengthened our picquets, manned the stone barricades, and fortified ourselves with whisky : but the night passed, with no more disturbance than the meehing of goats down in the valley below. So perhaps, after all, Rashid bin Harib's assessment of his news was sound.

The next morning Haugh and Gray set up their camp-chairs under a Land-Rover canopy and sent me off on patrol. I took with me a platoon of the Muscat Regiment, two mortar sections, and a R.A.F. officer who vicariously reinforced my patrol by at least two pairs of rocket-firing aircraft. We bundled into Land-Rovers and bounced away to battle. We were anxious about mines, so we kept off the track; this meant that our progress was at a ponderous walking pace, easing ourselves over the boulders and down and up the gullies like a dignified cavalcade of hippopotami. In this way we covered some ten miles by mid-morning. Just as it was beginning to get hot, we descried through the gathering heat-haze a low brown hill which seemed to have whitish bushes growing on it.

All of a sudden these bushes vanished; and shortly afterwards the hill sprouted a group of little puffs of grey smoke. These were followed, first, by a remote "pop", and then by a whirring sound as of monstrous beetles winging overhead.

We were being shot at.

Mingling with this antique volley were a few ominous signs of more contemporary warfare : the whip-crack of high-speed bullets, which preceded the sound of the weapon's detonation. We slid our trucks down into a rocky dip, piled out, sent a picquet to seize the nearest height, set up our mortars, and got ready to fling the gauntlet back in Talib's teeth.

As we performed the frantic motions of preparing for action

66

I suddenly noticed my R.A.F. comrade puffing lobster-faced and keen, with his burden of radio, faithfully at my side as I scrambled up the slope to take a better look.

What the hell, I thought. To dislodge those antediluvian but patently determined marksmen from their fastness would take all day, by conventional military means. A bayonet charge, in the baked mid-morning of an Arab summer's day, across half a mile of boulder-strewn plain, would perish miserably before we were half way there—of sprained ankles and heat-stroke. A tactical chess-game, of manœuvre and counter-move, would eventually win the day, if we could gain a position which outflanked or overlooked our foes . . . but Napoleon himself would need hours for that, and we were after all only a patrol. I raised my eyebrows at my Air Force friend; he nodded back, murmured some esoteric dialect into his radio . . . we waited a while, then as if in response to a call to Mephistopheles we heard the distant whine of jets.

The thing worked!

In a moment we could see them; a pair of high-flying birds, circling. The ground controller muttered things into his microphone. He glanced at me : I gave him a nod.

Down came the Venoms, one behind the other, screaming like Valkyries. They swooped low over the enemy hill, two iron-clawed eagles, talons unsheathed—they checked at the bottom of their parabola, turned, soared up into the Empyrean . . . what a terrifying visitation, I thought, remembering what the extraction of a glass eye had done to simple savages in Rider Haggard's tale—I peered through my field glasses, looking for fleeing men, panic stricken, or perhaps praying paralysed to their ancestors——

I saw them. They were standing up in their breastworks, waving their weapons festively. I could hear them. They were cheering in derision.

Two weeks ago this show of force would have made its due impression, on people who had never in their lives even heard of aeroplanes. When the Field Force had encountered a little indiscipline among the people of Ibri, the arrival of the Oil Company's pacific aircraft had had a most calming effect. But now, to our chagrin, we found our bluff called. The wild men of Oman had by now had plenty of aeroplanes flying over them, buzzing them, dropping leaflets, shooting holes in unoccupied forts. They were well inoculated.

So there they were, not cringing, not flinging their arms away in panic—not even taking cover, but cheering the skill of the pilots. It needed no more than another exchange of glances between myself and the airman; a few more muttered words in his microphone. The Venoms came screaming in again; the insolent Arabs cheered—then we heard a spitting sound, the whole of their hill sparkled with little flashes like fireworks as the cannon shells struck home—there followed a noise like a couple of dozen jumping crackers and the hill fell quiet.

Haughcol continued to probe into Suleiman's underbelly, but common sense restrained it from making any direct onslaught on the back door of Oman until some significant progress had been made by the main force from Fahud. They were facing some difficulty, in the shape of a determined bunch of men securely lodged in a craggy mountain overlooking the way to Nizwa— a far more formidable obstacle than the one we of Haughcol had obliterated. So we waited, day by day, probing deeper and deeper but not committing our modest force to the gage of battle, while we waited for the news that the main attack had broken through.

The collapse when it came was complete. Suddenly we heard that the enemy front before Nizwa had been burst; the Scotsmen, by a daring midnight leopard-leap, had captured the recalcitrant crag; an attack by my Venoms on the fortifications of Mutti induced the keepers of Suleiman's fortresses to sue for peace; a man came belting down the road from Izki assuring us of the undying loyalty of the good folk of that town to His Highness the Sultan.

We had won. Oman was ours—or rather, the Sultan's.

We drove delirious with victory through the surly populaces of village after village, bedraggled-looking red flags drooping out of windows, black crows of women staring fascinated at their first sight of European men.

One question remained, lurking awkwardly at the back of our minds behind the songs of triumph.

Where was Suleiman bin Himyar? Where was Talib?

Where, above all, was the Imam?

7

JASPER'S HORSE

WHERE, indeed, was the Imam? He was not to be seen this time, pacifically abdicating. Nor was Suleiman discernible, making his lordly homage to the conquering Sultan; and there was not the smallest vestige of Talib.

As we pursued our inquiries the lean grey rag-draped arms of the wise old men pointed a message that was increasingly unmistakable. They pointed to the east, and their aim was elevated noticeably from the horizontal. We followed their directions with reluctant eyes and saw that they all had the same message to impart.

The terrible three had gone up the Mountain.

We shaded our eyes with our hands and peered at the tableland heaving monstrously out of the distance, impregnable and secret. The British Brigadier who had been in charge of the conquest of Nizwa is said to have taken one look and announced that he would not dream of going anywhere near it with less than a Mountain Division, with Gurkhas. A division implies many thousand fighting men, complete with generous artillery and pack mules. We eyed our two or three hundred keen but scantily trained men, with their World War I rifles and not so much as a donkey to their name, and we shrugged our shoulders.

Furthermore, as soon as the Sultan's troops had re-installed themselves in Nizwa the whole of the foreign contingent withdrew, lest the liberal Press at home—which had wrought such damage during the Suez crisis—should gnash its teeth once more.

So away went the picturesque Carter with his Scouts, red scarves flying in the breeze; away went the Scots; and even the Air Force deserted us.

We were left, lonely and apprehensive, regarding the Jebel Akhdhar with growing distaste, fully knowing that until the elusive trio and their henchmen had gone for good there was small hope of peace for us and for the Sultan in this unfriendly land.

The Jebel Akhdhar is something of a geological show-piece. It was apparently formed by a block of limestone, about a mile thick and twenty miles across, suddenly thrusting itself up into the world above. This large stone had been lurking beneath more layers of limestone, several thousand feet deep. As the central lump forced its way upwards these layers opened out in much the same way as the petals of a flower, until the soaring massif stopped its ascent and the burst limestone strata were left leaning all around it looking like the points of a crown surrounding a mountainous bald pate.

These encircling slabs, of a roughly triangular shape, had their apexes at between seven and eight thousand feet, facing inwards and over-looking the flat top of the central plateau. The plateau was inhabited, with one fair-sized town and three or four smaller villages. The capital, Sharaija, tumbled down a thousand feet of sheer cliff in a cascade of terraces and rock-clinging houses, into a cavernous gorge. Water was abundant, the climate mild: the mountain harvests were more Mediterranean than Arabian, barley and grapes and walnuts. The people were ill-mannered, recluse, and addicted to the wine which they made from their grapes to while away the cold winter nights.

This much we learnt from the only source of information available on the Jebel Akhdhar: a book of travels by an obscure English explorer of the 1830s, which a Foreign Office official in Bahrein, anxious to help us in our predicament, had dug out of his library and sent us so that we could plan our next operations. This interesting but musty volume confirmed what we had already gathered from local inquiries—that the Jebel was apparently, for all practical purposes, invincible.

The only way to the foot of the central plateau was along one or another of a number of terrifying ravines gouged between the leaning triangular slabs. There was no point, it seemed, in trying to walk up any of these flanks despite their gentle slope, because when you got to the top you found yourself overlooking the plateau from the overhanging apex, with no possible way down. So the approach had to be along a ravine. But even when they had been reached, the mile-high sides were completely unscalable; they were more like the walls of a house than an ordinary mountainside. There were staircases built zigzag up the walls, like colossal fire-escapes, fashioned out of blocks of stone by some antediluvian inhabitants. To reach the top, you either walked upstairs or flew. There was positively no other way that anybody could see or discover from the most exhaustive researches.

From a mountaineering point of view, a cliff with a well-engineered staircase is a picnic. From a military point of view it is a calamity. Even the fanciful division of Gurkhas would have been constrained to walking up in single file, a mobile shooting-gallery for Talib's men on top—and this unpleasant prospect lay in wait beyond the approach ravine, in which two men and a boy, carefully sited, could probably hold an army at bay like Horatius at the Bridge.

There were other problems, touched on by the 1830 explorer but enlarged by our own observations. To climb up a mile of steps in the full glory of an Arabian summer—this was August—with the usual soldierly burdens of rations and armament, would cause the loss per person of between one and two gallons of sweat. This had to be replaced on the line of march somehow, or the entire invading force would collapse half way up. So unless some supply of water could be discovered and secured, a large number of pack animals would be needed to preserve the soldiers from literal dehydration. Then there was the question of reserve ammunition—more animals; blankets (for the nights up there were cold, however grilling the days)—yet more animals.

As we riffled through the traveller's archaic volume, and scanned the inscrutable faces of the mountain with our field glasses, it grew more and more obvious that to tackle Talib and his team on their own ground was going to be no easy undertaking. It was also obvious that we had to tackle them up there sooner or later, because they certainly would not come down by themselves.

While these anxious thoughts were going through our heads, we set about consolidating what we could, down at ground level where we could get at it.

Tariq, the Sultan's brother, had been appointed his vicar in the interior, and went about the countryside installing squads of the dubiously Loyal Tribesmen in the forts evacuated by Suleiman and Talib. In one or two cases the Government decided that it did not want to garrison the fort, so it blew it up instead. Stacks of explosive were placed at selected points inside, a fuse was lit, and with a mighty eruption the Castle of Izki soared sky-high in a thunderous cloud of pulverized mud brick. Up went the towers of Balad Sait, which had been so bold as to shoot at the Field Force; up went Suleiman's stronghold of Tanuf at the foot of the mountain; in an orgy of revenge the same sentence was passed on a house, a well, and a garden wall, which had given shelter in Nizwa to the musketeers lining the Field Force's retreat. The scent of cordite and powdered brick hovered on the air for many days. Where possible, Tariq selected a sheikh of uncertain affections and invited him to press the plunger— ensuring that a photograph was taken of him doing so, just in case it might ever be needed.

On our part, we built ourselves a new camp just outside Nizwa, and bucketed about the countryside looking for anybody who looked like Talib. And we put soldiers back into Nizwa fort.

Nizwa was the fort that had contemptuously shrugged off the anti-tank rockets of the R.A.F. Its main feature was a round tower like Windsor Castle, built of solid rock all through. There was a tunnel driven into it which let up to the top of the tower. Surrounding the top was a high mud wall, with embrasures for cannon, and a fire-step half way up for riflemen to shoot through loopholes. There were a couple of wells drilled through the solid part, which went down to a subterranean water supply, and there were two other holes which did not go all the way down and which had heavy wooden trap-doors. These were the prisoners' quarters. A prisoner was lowered down on a rope, the rope was pulled up, and the trap-door banged shut; and there he could be conveniently forgotten until he no longer mattered, when he was hoisted out again feet first.

The Fort was therefore entirely impregnable; with its own water supply, all it needed was sufficient food to withstand a siege. The heaviest artillery on earth would make no impression on its solid bulk, and nobody could hope to climb up its sides. The previous garrison had surrendered when the Field Force left, because they could see small point in bothering to hang on— when the army had gone there was not much glory to be earned by sitting on top of a pile of rock waving the Sultan's flag, even if Talib could not get at them. So they surrendered; and had been well treated. Now they were back again, peering down through their loopholes and gun-ports at the city beneath them. Nizwa town was a jumble of self-contained fortified boroughs, each inhabited by a particular tribe, and each turning is well-battlemented back on its neighbour. Surrounding the city was a green lake of palm-groves and fields of millet, lucerne, indigo and wheat; and supreme and alone over all was the great round tower.

During all this recreation the Jebel Akhdhar loomed ominous in our thoughts and on the horizon. And rapidly making of it his own private playground was that unusual Yorkshire airman, Jasper, now marvellously transmuted into an Arabian mercenary.

Jasper had retired from the R.A.F. at a decent retiring age, had promptly bought a khaki hat—which was just as revolting to look at as his blue one had been—and joined the Sultan's army. During the operations for the recapture of Nizwa he was generally to be seen striding around the battlefield, shillelagh in hand and waving an imperious red Government flag, summoning the tribes to submit in the Sultan's name. These enterprises brought him little response but a shower of lead. Undaunted, almost as soon as the round tower was in the Sultan's hands Jasper vanished from sight, to re-emerge a day or two later looking dusty, slightly shaken, but with a new glint in his eyes. He had been tackling the mountain fortress. He had captained a gaggle of assorted tribesmen in a hair-raising sally up one of the canyons. With blood-chilling war-cries, he told us, and guns going off in all directions, and brandishing a forest of red flags, the enthusiastic host charged off into the mouth of the gorge. But as the stark rock walls closed in, and the light of day was eclipsed to a spectral twilight, and their jubilant yells floated back down to them in melancholy echo, their élan evaporated. It turned out that they had thought the village which they were to plunder was a mere mile or so round a corner, but the blank sheer face of the plateau came into view and the guide pointed skywards and the appalled army silently melted away.

Jasper abandoned brute force and tried a more subtle approach. Hiring a donkey and a small boy he went up another ravine, alone, to try to locate the enemy picquets. He spent the night a rock or two below a nest of rebels, listening to them talking and cooking their meal; then, his mission done, he strode back down again, Bo-wood camera-box a-swinging.

This was the basis of our first serious attempt to find out more about the formidable altitude which separated us from Talib and his crew. I was invited to lead a small patrol, which was to investigate just what this mountain was really like; where it was penetrable, and where it was quite impossible. I was given a force of twelve men, Jasper, and some donkeys.

For Jasper had become regimental donkey-man. He had shown a peculiar sympathy with those charming animals. He enlisted a squadron of donkey-boys who became known as Jasper's Horse, and he recruited a number of great black mountain asses. These beasts were almost as big as mules, and were bred for the Jebel Akhdhar—no ordinary moke could get up it, even unladen, but these were sure-footed, muscular, and tractable. Jasper chose the biggest and blackest for his personal use, and he rode about the camp on it looking like Alexander on Bucephalus.

Jasper's donkeys adored him, and he tended them like a shepherd. He spent hours in his tent stitching together saddlery and harness—one of the many odd things about Jasper was his complete sailmaker's equipment : huge curved needles, lumps of beeswax, a monster thimble and yards and yards of sailcloth. With these he upholstered his donkeys.

At about this time Jasper hewed himself a new walking-stick. A gnarled bludgeon, knobbly as a Highlander's, it was made of Itm-wood. "Itm by name," said Jasper, "and 'it 'em by nature." He did, too. With his Harry Lauder walking-sticks, and his own private brand of malt whisky sent out to him by the case all the way from its obscure Strathspey distillery to the foot of the Jebel Akhdhar, Jasper was a memorable man.

Bob Warner, that elderly but determined man who had driven through the flooded salt-marsh to Tarif, had also retired (but at least he had retired from the *army*), and joined our merry band. He became a one-man headquarters, running the transport, the workshops, the signals, the cook-house, the buglers and the pay. He was also our quartermaster in his spare time, and never was there so zealous a custodian of stores. He was right, of course, in the way all Q.M.s are irrefutably right: as long as the stuff was safe in his stores, he had it in stock; if he issued it out, he no longer had it; and it was a poor quartermaster who had nothing in his stores.

The various disparate elements which had comprised Haughcol and the Sultan's contingent in the main Fahud assault had by now coalesced into a comparatively coherent whole under the benign colonelcy of Colin Maxwell. Maxwell had joined the Sultan quite by accident, while on his way to Borneo or somewhere, at the time of the abortive gathering of tribes to expel Turki from Buraimi, and he had been in his service ever since. He shared with Eric Johnson that indefinable sympathy with Arab soldiery which owed nothing to the Seven Pillars of Wisdom and sacrificed nothing to military principles, but he was large of girth and arthritic of hip and was unable to play a very forward part in the mountainous proceedings which now preoccupied us. However, he planned and encouraged; and we were also privileged to receive a flying visit from our monumentally imperturbable Chief of Staff, Pat Waterfield, a Medician sort of man and as many-counselled as Ulysses.

So one evening I found myself huddled with my twelve soldiers in a narrow rocky bowl, surrounded by cliffs so high that it was like the bottom of a mine-shaft, and nestling close against Jasper and his donkeys. My task was to reconnoitre this particular route to the top of the Jebel Akhdhar; peer over the lip of the plateau, just so that we could say we had got to the top; and come down again. The last time a military force had made the Green Mountain, so we were told, was a thousand years before, when a human tide of Persians had flooded up from the other side, losing frightful numbers of men but still having enough left by the time they got to the top to be able to clobber the inhabitants. If this legend was true, there was something mildly historic about the present expedition.

The night passed quietly enough. Our only anxiety was that Jasper's Horse would start to bray, for once one began the whole lot would join in a donkey's chorus bellowing up the face of the cliff and arousing the entire population of the Jebel. But they held their tongues, like the well-disciplined beasts they were, and when my party began its climb at dawn the donkeys said not a word.

The first few hundred feet of the ascent clambered up a hairpinning staircase of stone steps, which led eventually on to a sloping ridge where the path laboured on until it staggered across in a diagonal climb up the main face of the plateau. If there had been any enemy sentinels at the top of this first flight of steps we would have been helpless; there was no way up except the stairs, and a man with a few rounds of ammunition could have hidden himself behind a suitable boulder and stopped us moving at all. Nor would the R.A.F. have been any help; the steps rose out of the very source of the ravine at the foot of the plateau, and the only aircraft capable of doing anything would have been a Stuka—piloted by a Kamikazi. There was an ominous black boulder near the head of the staircase, three or four hundred feet up, and we eyed it with considerable distaste as we toiled our way towards it.

As soon as we made the top of the steps and got on to the more open side of the rising ridge we realized that we had not been too soon. We spotted them at the same time they spotted us: a group of rangy-looking men with skirts tucked up, leaping like goats from rock to rock down the ridge towards us. For a moment there was a prickly pause as they gaped at us and we, breasting the last of the steps and out of breath, blinked at them—then they were gone, and from a pile of boulders came puffs of smoke and the beetle-whirr of bullets, with now and then the alerting crack of a modern weapon. We had only just beaten them to the black rock.

But here we could move. Two or three of my soldiers nipped up the slope to the right of the track, dodging between the boulders till they gained a rocky perch overlooking where the snipers had gone to ground. A Bren gun sputtered a burst or two and we heard no more of the mountaineers. A mountain Arab is as tenacious as a rock-plant when he holds a position above his target but when he is outflanked and overlooked in his turn he feels naked and ashamed and rapidly makes himself scarce. This was a tactic which we used as often as we could, when we realized the psychological effect of looking down on our opponents, but there were so few places on the approaches to the mountain where we could manœuvre at all that its exercise was limited. At any rate, this small battle had cleared our path of human obstacles and we continued our trudge unmolested.

Nothing else happened at all on the way up. We found a rock-basin holding a goaty supply of water, where we rested and refreshed ourselves; then we plodded on up the endless steps across the face of the cliff, until we rounded a corner and the track threaded along the edge of a ravine. Here the path—never more than a yard wide—clung desperately to the side of the precipice, with a steep rise above it to the right and a sheer drop into space on the left. Here, very obviously, was no way for a military patrol to proceed. I made a swift redeployment to investigate the terrain away from this death-trap, upwards to the brow of the plateau; I had breasted the slope and was some considerable distance above the cliff-hanging track when a crackle of gunfire below and in front broke the peace of the morning for the first time since we had warned off our reception committee on the ridge. At the same moment I looked around for the rest of my patrol and found that by masterly tactics I had contrived to outflank myself—there was not a soul within sight. I had, in the military phrase, dropped a clanger. Here was the patrol leader alone and alarmed on the edge of the Jebel Akhdhar, and there, presumably, was his patrol, some hundreds of feet below him, embroiled with an enemy picquet on the main line of march. I made a mental memo to brush up my Arabic before trying any more tactics, and slithered back down the way I had come until I was again at the point where the track began to snake its perilous way along the precipice.

There I found most of my patrol, to my huge relief, looking reproachfully at me and asking for intelligible orders; and at the same moment my native officer, Ali Mohammed, came galloping back round the bend ahead, with his face covered in dust, a shaken look in his eyes, and a frightening tale on his lips—he had made his way along the track, he said, completely misunderstanding my orders and imagining that I was always just out of sight beyond, when a jack-in-the-box with a turbaned head popped up over a rock as he turned a corner. For a long moment the two stared at each other—both equally appalled—then Ali Mohammed drew his pistol and fired at the turban, the turban simultaneously let off his rifle and vanished from sight, and Ali, realizing that it was impossible that I could have gone before him, had withdrawn with considerable speed.

By this time the sun was beginning to show definite signs of being afternoon, and it was imperative that we get back to the bottom of the mountain before nightfall. We turned our faces downwards, making better speed with the force of gravity working with us instead of against us, and before dark I was reunited with Jasper and his donkeys and gratefully enjoying a tin mug of his special Highland malt. We had achieved no spectacular victory but we had learnt some precious lessons, and we had lifted at least a corner of the veil of the Jebel Akhdhar.

The next months were for Jasper and myself completely devoted to this infernal lump of rock. In honour of our dedication we both grew beards. Three more times I took up small groups of men, supported invaluably both materially and morally by Jasper and his long-eared friends.

Once we tried the impossible gorge which Jasper had assaulted with his flag-waving rabble, reached the spring which was our objective, drank, rested, and turned to go—to be set upon by a furious volley hurled at us by a frustrated ambush who had been patiently lying in wait just above the water. The noise of their shots in that confined space was like an artillery bombardment. Luckily we could see the cave where they were firing from, so I grabbed a Bren gun from a protesting gunner and aimed tracer bullets at the roof of the cave, so that they ricocheted around inside. With gratifying dispatch three brown-robed blackbeards shot out from their cover and belted away uphill as if the hounds of hell were after them. We were lucky on that patrol—if we had been caught upstream with the ambush below us we would have been most unhappy. As it happened our only damage was a soldier with a wrecked foot.

On a couple of other patrols we tried a route going up from Suleiman's erstwhile capital, Tanuf with the exploded fort. For these we had a guide named Darwish, who assured us that he knew just the way to the very heart of Suleiman's stronghold which avoided all ravines, cliffs, staircases and narrow places—merely a pleasant walk uphill for two or three days. But Darwish had his own peculiar way of imparting information. He was a long lean grizzled man of the hills, like an ancient mountain goat, and his dialect of Arabic was as obscure as a Highlander's English. For one thing, he did not share our concept of left and right; as he used the terms they related less to the two hands of the body than to the rising and setting of the sun. He had, moreover, only one word for "yes" and "no"—a kind of grunt, highly expressive but hard to interpret. For "yes" he said "hu-huh" and shook his head from side to side; for "no", he said "hu-huh" and nodded enthusiastically. And although he was able to count, he found difficulty in relating the numerals to the sum he was trying to convey, so that when, for instance, we asked him how many watercourses we would cross on this route of his, he held up four fingers and said "three"; asked how many days to the summit, he waggled three fingers and said "two".

After many prolonged and patient interviews with Darwish we thought we had made contact. He would not, he said, lead us on our reconnaissance, for reasons of health, but he would accompany the rearguard and would be available for consultation whenever required. So we had to make sure of our way beforehand, and then try it, with Darwish guiding us from behind like the Duke of Plaza-Toro.

Up we went. I was leading, as I had attended the briefing conferences, but I grew increasingly puzzled. Although I was, I thought, following his instructions minutely the route bore no resemblance at all to his description. Far from being an open climb, it began up a narrow corridor of cliffs and then started abruptly to wind its way up the side of a towering precipice, getting narrower and more vertiginous with every step. Nor was it long before the popping and cracking and whirring of musketry sounded around us, echoing wonderfully from towering heights. Clearly, either I was up the pole or Darwish was round the bend. Pursued eagerly by showers of shot, which happily did no more than whistle over our respectfully bowed heads, down we came again. I was opening my mouth to ask Darwish what the hell, when I saw him wagging his hoary head and looking at me as if I was unfit to lead a dance let alone a patrol.

Shaking a palsied hand he pointed to the other wall of the gorge we had just left. "Not this side!" he croaked, nodding his head emphatically. "The other side!" So the mistake was, after all, mine.

Shortly afterwards we went up the other side and found it to be indeed as he described it : no more than an extended rock-climb, over open ground for the most part, taking us up to a peak at eight thousand feet from where we could gaze down the far side of the Jebel Akhdhar to the distant sea. We had, however, not broken into Suleiman's fastness; we had merely reached his back door. Facing us was a narrow neck where two gorges fell away, one towards the sea and one inland to join the Tanuf ravine, and astride this col was a formidable natural barbican, from which defiant popping sounds could be heard; field glasses revealed a multitude of turbans among the rocks.

On this expedition we were pursued at a safe distance by some hundred or so of Tariq's tribesmen, who were supposed to act as reinforcements in case my reconnaissance patrol came up against anything in the way of a strongpoint. I also had with me a jolly ginger-haired pink-kneed R.A.F. officer called George Gardner, nobly staggering uphill beside me with a wireless set on

F   81

his back; for the Air Force had by this time agreed to help us if in need.

There, in front, was decidedly a strongpoint; here was I, with my two sections of soldiers, and behind us, snaking interminably along the path, were my reinforcements—Arabs of all ages from twelve to sixty, dressed in all manner of colours, bearing arms which would have delighted a museum curator but which gave me the horrors. When they caught up with my patrol I held a council of war, and it was resolved that we should try it if the aeroplanes gave us fire support. I turned to Gardner.

Gardner muttered into his microphone, reminiscent of Haughcol, and before long a ponderous four-engined bomber came throbbing overhead. Gardner passed on my request for a blanket of fire from the bomber's machine guns, which we could see sticking out of its nose like an unpleasant insect's proboscis. The four engines throttled back, the leviathan zoomed over our heads towards the target, we held our breath—there were two or three depressed-sounding pops from this dreadnought of the skies, Gardner turned to me dispiritedly and said, "his guns are jammed", and the thing turned for home and that was the last we saw of it.

Gardner had one more card up his sleeve. He conjured up a pair of Venoms, those jet fighters which had served us so well before; after a long wait, when the day was well advanced, they arrived from Sharjah. Gardner hastily described the target— "ridge with two tits" was his picturesque indication—the Venoms soared, hovered, swooped, opened up, and with a hellish clatter of exploding cannon-shells and volcanic clouds of dust they hammered the ridge whereon we sat. By God's good grace none of us—soldier nor tribesman—was hit, although we were all sitting around in the open to watch the show.

As the Venoms swept off home, doubtless well satisfied with their marksmanship, it was obvious from the approach of evening that we could make Jasper's camp—donkeyloads of food, bedding, water and whisky—by nightfall if we set off at once, or make boldly for the barbican and hope to carry it with our now thoroughly sceptical camp-followers. The prize was not worth the odds. Even if we took the place we would have to leave it again—there were neither plans nor resources to support a permanent outpost of our own up there, and there were no means whatever of exploiting it. So home we went, having learnt—if nothing else—not to trust aeroplanes, and how to understand Darwish.

8

THE MELANCHOLY MOUNTAINEER

A CAVERNOUSLY gloomy man called John Clarke joined us during these escapades. He had a tall lean body and a melancholy black moustache, and he spoke in a mournful monotone like a Requiem Mass. He had a lugubrious sense of humour and was indifferent to danger, and he rapidly became one of our biggest assets.

The Powers—notable among whom was the all-powerful Waterfield—had decided by now that the time for playing around on the mountainside had come to an end and we must try to do something memorable. They accordingly devised a master plan involving two whole companies of our own troops, two more companies of Carter's Scouts (who bowled merrily down again to Oman in their bouncing Land-Rovers), several hundred hirsute Arab irregulars led personally by Tariq, and as many aeroplanes as the R.A.F. could spare.

The plan was as follows.

The Trucial Oman Scouts were to walk up the two triangular slabs on either side of that gorge where Ali Mohammed had had his brush with the spring-loaded sentry. There they would establish picquets, several thousand feet up in the air. I would take our own two companies, together with John Clarke who, although far older and wiser a soldier, was new to this particular game, and supported by Jasper's indispensable donkeys. Having captured a water-hole, which the Powers had discerned on an aerial photograph a little beyond where I had reached the time before, we would set up a base, through which the plunder-hungry horde of Arabs would charge on to the open plateau top and sack a village or two. In order to discourage any of Talib's men who might be rash enough to oppose this pillage, we had a pink-kneed blue-cap and—hovering somewhere out of sight—his aeroplanes.

The plan swivelled on one lynch-pin. The water-hole had not only to be captured: before that, it had to exist, as more than a round black blob on an aerial photograph, and if it existed it had to be accessible from our route. For an army on that mountainside marched on its water-bottles.

All began well. The Scouts shinned up into outer space, we plodded up the gorge, the R.A.F. dropped loads of bombs into the head of the ravine to disintegrate anybody who might have been lurking behind the black rock guarding the first flight of steps. We pressed on. As we began to emerge on to the sloping ridge we were fired at from a knob half way across the cliff face which we had to traverse; the aeroplanes clobbered the knob and the snipers desisted for a while. We reached the rock basin where my patrol had refreshed itself on our first expedition, but the unchristian defenders had since filled it up with donkey dung and other nastiness so we had to make do with our water-bottles until we captured that questionable but vital water-hole. Jasper had water on his donkeys but it was only enough to ensure that we could get back down the mountain again without dying of thirst, should the plan go awry.

By nightfall we had reached the place where the path began to creep edgeways along the ravine. I poked a tentative nose round the corner and at once I felt a violent crash on the rock six inches away from my crutch and simultaneous stings as from a swarm of bees around the groin: as I bobbed down out of sight I could see a cluster of turbans ensconced behind a boulder a few hundred yards further along the track, and it was their greeting shot that had exploded against the mountainside, missing my person by a handsbreadth and peppering me with bits. Clearly, to teeter along that ledge was still no way for a military expedition; our only way forward was off the track and clambering up the bare brow of the plateau, as I had tried before.

It was now nearly dark, and rock-clambering would be swift suicide, so I staked out sentries and settled down for a chilly and boulder-cradled night, intending to press on in the morning. John Clarke left me, just as the stars came out, and made his way gingerly a few hundred yards downhill to discuss something with Jasper who had followed us as closely as his donkeys would allow.

Cramp and thirst kept sleep away till dawn, when I unstuck my eyes, mustered my men, and looked around for the sad-faced Clarke. He was nowhere at hand. I spent precious time slithering down to Jasper, and Jasper said that Clarke had left him after only a short sojourn. We shared an unpleasant moment. We remembered that the night had once been ripped apart by musketry from further above us, and had assumed it to be either exuberance or hysteria on the part of the Jebel's defenders—now it took on a more alarming complexion. But the missing major had not passed through my post, so how had he got above us to spark off that fusillade? It was impossible—there was only the one track, and we were astride it.

Tariq, whose noble bulk was visible just below us well to the forefront of his mob, bearing on its ample shoulder a Bren gun, scattered his men scampering all over the hillside to our right flank, to discover if Clarke had lost his way and injured himself. He was nowhere. There was thus only one other place he could possibly be and that was on our left; and our left flank was a leap into space.

Perhaps mistakenly, from a strict military point of view, we—Jasper, Tariq, myself and troops—were by now far more concerned about the possible fate of John Clarke than we were with the extremely hairy plan we had come up here to accomplish. We searched everywhere, desperately, until at the end it was dismally clear that John Clarke was dead—there was nowhere he could be except down that ravine, and the only way down there was to fly; or to fall. He must have slipped off the edge in the dark on his way up from Jasper to me. There was quite simply no other solution—short of bodily assumption.

By the time we reached this conclusion the violation of the Jebel Akhdhar had dropped to second place. It was, as planned, no more than a punitive or bravado raid, and to most of us the search for John Clarke took priority over tribal looting. We had at any rate reached the bottom of our water, the cool of the morning had passed, and we weighed the choice : to go home plunderless, or press forward in a mad gamble on finding the notional water-hole. "Election makes not up on such conditions." The R.A.F. offered a few encouraging swoops over the brow of the plateau but failed to persuade us. We bade a sad farewell to John Clarke and made our funereal way homewards. We had learnt one lesson : the impossibility of conducting offensive operations on the Green Mountain without a secure water supply, or a bigger water-train than we had donkeys or containers to transport. When the water-hole of the planners was eventually located, long afterwards, it was found lurking at the bottom of a crevice, accessible only to mountain goats and unknown except as a distant prospect even to the inhabitants of the Jebel.

For the next day or two patrols of neutral goat-men scoured the hillside for traces of the missing Clarke, aircraft flew low over the track and the gorge looking for any sign of human life—and military scouts waited at all the feasible exits from the mountain stronghold in case by some miracle he had found another way down. At the end of it all Colin Maxwell was on the point of composing a telegram of condolences to his next of kin when the man himself walked glumly into one of the ground patrols—looking more gloomy than usual, but intact. After the celebrations—we greeted him as one literally returned from the dead, which he was—he told us his tale.

When he left me, at dusk, he called on Jasper to discuss a few details of the morrow's dispositions. One or two swigs of the special Strathspey warmed him for the return journey uphill; somehow on the way he strayed from the path, but to the right, not to the left where the ravine lay in wait. He blundered on, over boulders and crevices, feeling sure that my advanced post was only just ahead, when he suddenly found himself the target of a hail of bullets. This was the volley we had heard during the night. Realizing that he had gone too far, the errant Clarke at once assessed his situation, alone and bewildered on the midnight mountain-top : any downward direction would surely take him, in time, to the foot of the Jebel and to safety, whereas any other line would probably take him further into the bosom of the enemy. So downwards he went. This tack took him to the edge of a vast empty drop into space—but having chosen his line he pursued it. How he got down he was never able to say, but an amnesic slide on his rump took him to the bottom of the very ravine where we had thought his broken body to lie. By the time our search parties and aeroplanes, peering dizzily into the canyon, had begun to look for him, Clarke was already staggering down the gorge to its mouth. Half drunk with thirst, he saw tortoises and other odd things on the way, he told us. The mystery of his midnight descent of a sheer precipice remains locked to this day in his subconscious.

During these days it was my lot to report to the Minister of the Interior after our patrols, so that he could convey his own impressions of our enterprise to the Sultan. The Minister for Internal Affairs was called Father Christmas, because of a flamboyant marvel of a beard, delicately redolent of incense, which stuck out in all directions like the white rays of a misty sun. He wore a plain white gown and a cloak of diaphanous black muslin, and on top of the lot was a huge fantastical hat. This was of white linen wound into a curious ogive shape like the Temple of the Tooth; it leant over at the top, and swayed in the breeze. This turban was his filing cabinet. It fluttered with documents of different kinds, stuck methodically into its regular folds.

Father Christmas had an impediment in his otherwise melodious speech. His tongue led an independent life of its own, intruding into the conversation with all sorts of extra labio-dental sounds; and he had a tendency to spoonerisms (Arabic spoonerisms are spectacular). So unless one knew him well, an interpreter was needed, however fluent one's Arabic; this job was carried out by a confidential secretary, called Electric-whiskers after his heroic attempt to emulate his master's beard—this one looked as if a couple of thousand volts were being sparked through it.

The entire Ministry of the Interior, in those hectic days, was a tiny chamber in the great fort of Nizwa, where Father Christmas sat enthroned on a rolled-up bedding valise—ready for instant flight, we thought maliciously, but this was unworthy as he was a courageous old fellow. And from this bedding-roll, with his files on his head, he governed Oman with imperious serenity.

Following the fiasco of the plunder-raid, the Sultan's military advisers turned to the Royal Air Force for a plan of attack. The water problem had defeated us; what could the Boys in Blue suggest? R.A.F. Headquarters went into labour, and in due course brought forth a Plan to end all plans. The thirst-bound soldiery would this time merely be decoys to entice the Jebel defenders into the open; then the airmen would go in and drop enormous bombs on them and blow them all to bits. This was the essence of the most calamitous stratagem of the whole campaign.

Using the same route as the one where we had lost John Clarke, because we—Jasper and I, donkeys and troops—were getting to know it fairly well, a ponderous column was to make its way conspicuously one afternoon up the approach ravine. It was to pass the evening noisily at the bottom of the steps; and it was to creep away back down again during the night. Then, as the sun rose on a hillside swarming with Talib's men all exposed in battle array to receive our assault, waves of bombers would fly over and drop 1,000-lb. bombs all over them.

All went more or less as planned, except that the decoy column met some opposition because by this time the defenders were getting as accustomed to our choice of this route as we were. My job on this jamboree was to lead a small picquet up one of the flanking slabs, to protect the column in the ravine from premature enemy attention. Just as we were settling into position one of my men took a shot in the leg, and we were all rather accurately sniped at until we found the range of the marksman and winkled him out of his hide.

A recurrent nightmare on all our mountain expeditions was the thought of a badly wounded man. Off the trodden track, donkeys and stretcher-bearers were as useless as ambulances—this was hand-and-knee, mountain-rescue stuff. I was lucky in all my forays that I was never presented with a serious casualty; we were not equipped to carry a man with a broken back down two or three thousand feet of tumbled boulders and walls of rock. On this day my stricken soldier had only a flesh wound, and he was trundled down to the doctor by some porters who had brought up jerricans of water for us. They had drunk most of the water themselves, but their return journey was not wasted.

The parallel picquet on the slab the other side of the gorge had two or three brisk exchanges of fire, one with some enemy on a ledge above them and another by mistake with their own comrades in the ravine below, but neither engagement caused them any damage.

On the way down, however, during the secret withdrawal, the night was suddenly made hideous by gunfire. One of our soldiers let off his Bren gun as he stumbled over a rock, almost severing the leg of a Royal Marine corporal who was accompanying the force : the corporal died on the way to hospital. He was the only mortal casualty, apart from one donkey. Jasper's right-hand donkey man, too, had taken a bullet through his own right hand; and that was about the total tally. My own picquet, somehow, contrived to get itself down the face of the slab in pitch darkness, more or less carrying me with it—at one stage I seemed to be feeling my sightless way down a human staircase of heads, shoulders, and knees; we dared not strike even a match for fear of betraying the Plan. By the time we set foot on level ground our uniforms were in shreds and our skins almost as tattered. I decided that I loathed the Jebel Akhdhar.

But punctual dawn saw us drawn up happily on the plains, peering up at the towering face of the cliff-side where all the flower of Oman was supposed to be arrayed to meet our attack . . . over came the bombers, down came the bombs, and they were the biggest bombs I had ever seen—marching silently in giant strides up the mountainside was a rank of mushroom clouds like small atomic explosions, then came another rank, until the whole face of the Jebel Akhdhar was obscured with dust and smoke—then after a minute of suspense came the detonations, the thunder of a thousand drums rolling and reverberating down the slopes towards us. It was most impressive.

Later that day Tariq sent up scouting goat-men to count the corpses and report on the wailing of bereaved mountain women.

They came down again and told us that all was quiet. The defenders had not been near the target area at all, but had been watching the fireworks as interestedly from above as we had been from below.

And that was the last Plan to capture the Green Mountain from the cockpit of an aeroplane. It was borne upon the Powers that there was only one way to do it and that was to put guns and soldiers up on top. Soldiers could not get up there by simply walking up the stairs, unless they were supported by a long enough animal train to sustain a three or four days' effort—there was to be no more of the sort of plan which hinged on imaginary or inaccessible water-holes. All the other routes, moreover, had by this time been exhaustively surveyed by pedestrian or aerial reconnaissance, and all seemed even less feasible than our favourite. Any other scheme was manifestly mad—there was, so far as human eyes and camera lens could see, no other way to get there at all, except by balloon.

As these sober assessments were being made, the comparatively cool winter season came to an end and the stoking heat of summer made active mountaineering impossible. The Powers had no choice but to leave the dreadful triad in peace on their hilltop, and consolidate what we had at ground level, until the next cool season : when perhaps somebody else might have thought of what to do.

By the end of the winter, moreover, it had become more and more apparent that we were going to be fully extended maintaining what control we had over the foothills and plains around the skirts of the Jebel Akhdhar, where ran the vital main artery to the oil camp at Fahud, dominated by villages and towns of the tribes of Suleiman bin Himyar and the Imam. Talib's first pinpricks had made us wince during our early mountain climbs, and by the end of winter he had not only made it impossible to spare enough troops for our own offensive activities but forced us to cry for outside help. The Trucial Oman Scouts stationed a company permanently at our side at Izki, and the Royal Marines sent us some magnificent N.C.O.s who had become bored with shipboard duties and volunteered for the nearest war. This happened to be ours at the time, so they came to us, as training staff and patrol leaders. These men were in every way splendid representatives of their splendid service. Later the volunteer element was submerged and Marines were posted to us willy-nilly, with a consequent decline in enthusiasm; but men like Sergeant Pugh and Corporal Lonsdale, who were attached to me, were each worth a couple of dozen ordinary soldiers. The Jollies taught our men, and led them, by a mixture of impeccable personal example and lucid parade-ground phraseology, unmistakable to a Hottentot, and their lack of Arabic was no sort of hindrance. The corporal who was accidentally killed on the bombing-raid was one of this fine small band of men.

The first indication that Talib's warriors were not cowering craven and dispirited on their plateau was the ambush and abduction of an oil company driver, pursuing his peaceful way past Izki towards Fahud. Then we had a truck blown up on a mine, which we were inclined to think had been left over from the previous campaign; but when other mines followed, in increasing profusion, it was no longer possible for us to adhere to this optimistic opinion. In order to secure the thoroughfare through Izki, a company was sent there to erect a temporary camp and patrol the ambush-prone foothills and deter layers of mines. This camp was shot at one night from the very hills it was supposed to control, one soldier was killed, and the gay tented compound quickly burrowed into the earth. We found ourselves rapidly adopting an altogether less cavalier approach to mountain warfare.

Meanwhile the mountain top was being steadily reinforced. Young men vanished from the villages—Izki, Mutti, Balad Sait: driving through them we could see babies, women, and wizened old men, nobody else. Nor was Saleh bin Issa sitting idly by; that Prince of the Sharqiya whose brother Ibrahim was still dolorously thumbing through his Koran in the Sultan's prison. In the noisy oil town of Dammam, on the Persian Gulf coast of Saudi Arabia, he was rounding up likely young lads, collecting cash, and accumulating weapons and other warlike stores, to hasten our departure.

The Melancholy Mountaineer

While we were building up Izki and other garrisons on the inland side of the Jebel Akhdhar, the seaward side was left unwatched except by the old mud forts of the Sultan's Nelson-eyed deputies. This became the principal supply route of Talib's commissariat, in which more than one of the Sultan's satraps profitably dabbled.

One particular consignment of men and matériel was a masterpiece of daring—or of accurate appreciation. It came within a hair of turning the tables on the Sultan's forces, and gave us nightmares for months. This coup was engineered by Saleh bin Issa, who was cleverly managing to keep out of the way while all the shooting was going on but ensuring for himself a place in Paradise when the Imam ruled once more.

The first part of the plot was to accumulate the persons and goods on the Oman side of the desert. The conspirators shipped these in by dhow to Sharjah, with the capable assistance of a senior State official, who stored them in a building attached to the ruler's gorgonzola palace. There were some forty tough and well-drilled youths, who were to serve as a hard core for the woollier warriors currently holding the passes. These thugs belonged to a bellicose tribe from the extreme depths of Saleh's principality, and they were fine material. A formidable arsenal accompanied them : mortars and bombs, anti-aircraft machine guns, boxes and boxes of mines, and a radio set with which the Jebel Akhdhar was to keep in touch with its supporters' club in Dammam. This gathering took place right under the nose of the Trucial Oman Scouts; but it was no part of their mandate to be suspicious of the Ruler of Sharjah, on whose side they were supposed to be.

The next stage of the plan was to smuggle the reinforcements out of Sharjah, into Oman Proper, and up to the Jebel Akhdhar. The coast was watched only by the Sultan's customs men and the somnolent guards of his governors. The customs men were in those days capable of lining their own pockets with legitimate revenue, but not of preventing professional and determined gun-running. The men and munitions were accordingly infiltrated piecemeal on hired pack-animals through the hills to the Indian

Ocean coast, where they gathered themselves together on the home side of the frontier post.

The conspirators next obtained a truck, and drove it openly and innocently along the main road through the customs post to rendezvous with the accumulating passengers and freight. For many days, travellers up and down the highway observed a broken-down lorry, its front axle spread convincingly in pieces around it, its passengers lolling under the trees or cooking rice. This was a common enough spectacle on that road, and nobody remarked that as the days went by the number of passengers increased, that they were to a man healthy young striplings of military age—a rarity in war-torn Oman, and that their baggage and belongings were wonderfully sprouting around them like mushrooms overnight.

After a few days the consignment was complete. The driver briskly reassembled his front axle, and the impudent lorry set off down the main thoroughfare with its incredible load of soldiers, mortars, mines and machine guns. It bowled unconcernedly along the highway, through towns and villages, under the guns of the Sultan's forts and doubtless past more than one army patrol. When it reached a point level with the Jebel Akhdhar it turned off the coast road and drove inland. This way to the Jebel was guarded closely by two strongholds, Rostaq (whence Talib had been evicted by Colin Maxwell two and a half years before) and Awabi, the latter being a fortress tucked hard against the foot of the mountain and overlooking the road where it finally disappeared into the cliffs.

The lorry charged along this road, bald-headed. At Rostaq it was challenged by the guards but blithely ignored them. Between Rostaq and Awabi one of our Land-Rovers passed it; the drivers exchanged friendly waves. At Awabi it was again challenged, execrated, shot at—but its driver jammed foot to floorboards, bounced madly over the boulders, and ran the blockade. Past this last hazard he was safe in mountain country. He finally pulled up at the foot of the plateau; the men and goods were off-loaded on to donkeys; and the whole evaporated up the face of the cliff. The intrepid lorry was ceremoniously set on fire. None of us knew the first thing about what had happened.

All Talib's eggs were in this one fantastic basket. Shortly after that our reconnaissance planes were greeted with ·5 machine guns, our camps were pelted with mortar bombs, our patrols were seen off by Saleh bin Issa's determined young men. The only discord in this fanfare of success was the radio. They never got through to Dammam, not once.

9

LIFE IN A HOLE

I z k i was perhaps the only place in the world in 1958 where one could consume Chicken Marengo followed by Compôte de Fruits au Kirsch, in a hole in the ground.

The holes were due to the epidemic of sniping which the camp had suffered since the beginning of the year. What was intended as a temporary enclave to deter ambushes was becoming bogged down in the introspective task of defending itself. Under each tent there was now a pit, from wall to wall and four or five feet deep, so that the inside of the tent was like a comfortable room. In these holes we lived, ate, slept, and amused ourselves when not trying to catch snipers. On a rock pinnacle overlooking the camp we built a machine-gun nest out of kerosene tins filled with earth.

The Chicken Marengo and Kirsch were due to Richard Anderson, who was O.C. of this haven of subterranean gourmandizing when my company was posted there. He was a globular man of bright scarlet countenance, prone to eruptions of choler which he strove heroically to contain—with varying success. He inspired great affection in his men, who called him "Major Drum" and learnt to turn their backs to the occasional tempest of temperament; he had a passion for Gilbert and Sullivan, an astonishing memory for the most recondite information, a deep devotion to the profession of arms—and a nicely cultivated palate. As the only other officer at Izki I bore the brunt of the whole mélange. And the delicate dishes, served by

Nizwa, capital of Oman. The great round tower dominates the whole city.

The Imam. The white turban is the badge of the holy men of Oman.

Suleiman Bin Himyar. With him are his two sons and a slave.

Riverside scene. Foothills of the Green Mountain loom in the background.

The road to Nizwa. The mountains are never far away.

(left) Sayid Tariq—he was a fine marksman and played a good hand of bridge. *(right)* The Interior Minister—we called him Father Christmas.

Suleiman and the Iman. The Lord of the Green Mountain wears a Kashmir shawl.

One of the ruins the R.A.F. knocked about a bit.

One of the gorges. Tanuf lies in ruins in the foreground.

Before our big guns came. These little ones could just get over
the crest.

Men of Oman. The tall thin one might be Darwish.

Maxwell *(left)* and Anderson *(right)*. Somehow they both fitted in one Land-Rover.

Intelligence officer Dennison (facing camera, white headdress) and friends.

Headquarters. Back row: No 2, Warner; No 3, Dennison; No 5, our Doctor. Front row: No 2, Maxwell; No 3, Smiley; No 5, author (in red balmoral).

Medals. Colonel David Smiley decorates a Baluch colour-sergeant.

a white-coated steward, partaken of to the airs of *The Gondoliers* and punctuated by explosions of Andersonian wrath and the sharper crack of bullets passing harmlessly over our underground banquet—these remain among my more indelible memories. Early every morning Anderson could be seen returning magisterially from the hills, a spherical figure in a blue polka-dot dressing gown, bearing under one arm a roll of paper and under the other a loaded sten gun which had been his only defence from assassination or emasculation as he squatted pensive among the rocks. He was braver than I was: I used to wait until it got dark in the evening, so that I could attend to nature closer to the camp's machine-guns.

Around the tents we built a wall. By the time it was up to its final height of five feet we could at last emerge from our dug-outs and live at ground level, unalarmed by the phut of bullets against its stony face.

The wall was built in an archaic though effective manner. A double row of pillow-sized boulders was laid along a line, with about six inches between rows. Gravel and pebbles were poured in to fill the gaps and liquid mud smeared overall to hold the layer in place. Then the process was repeated, layer after layer until the required height was reached. At the corners we erected round towers, five feet high like the wall, each housing half a dozen men and a machine-gun. The complete efficacy of this barricade—until the enemy mortars opened up later on—induced in us a rather defensive state of mind, but we made efforts to counter that by patrolling. We also laid trip-flares in likely approaches to where people might shoot at us, so that snipers on their way to snipe would set off a magnesium firework at which we had previously aimed our mortars and machine-guns. They used to go off almost every night, with an automatic accompaniment of wrath from our prepared weapons and from the O.C., but in most cases our optimistic burial parties the next morning found nothing but some tiny footprints and scattered fur suggesting an astonished rabbit or fox.

But our fifty-odd soldiers spent all of most days and half of most nights endeavouring to keep the road clear of mines.

During the early part of 1958 the mines became an imperial headache, pushing right out of our minds all thought of assaulting the Jebel or even beating up one or two villages. Our entire effort, physical and intellectual, was absorbed by this nuisance. We must run trucks up and down the roads—if we had been able to use camels or helicopters it would not have mattered, but we were completely dependent upon road transport. And at the height of the plague we lost two and sometimes three trucks blown up in one day. We had no wealth of lorries, and certainly none to spare, so this was developing for us into something like what the U-boat blockade was to Britain.

Not only the army suffered. The oil company enjoyed no immunity, nor did the occasional tradesman who tried the journey—they soon stopped—and many a camel and donkey was reduced to its component parts by unwisely putting a hoof in the wrong place.

Anderson was determined to leave no wounded vehicle as a standing sign of our discomfiture. Situated on the main road from Muscat to Nizwa and Fahud, we at Izki felt the full fury of the mine warfare, and Anderson insisted that all should be brought in. Every time we heard a convoy approaching from left or right, we held our breath. Sure enough, sooner or later came a dull bang, followed at once by a louder bang from Anderson—then out we went, hitched up the wreck to the back of our lorry and heaved it home. Eventually it was lumbered all the way down to Muscat where a junk-yard of shattered vehicles quickly accumulated.

There was one spectacular occasion when we loaded a blown-up Land-Rover on to a three-tonner and sent it on its way to the Muscat morgue. It had not gone two miles when we heard the usual dull thump and went out to find the three-tonner looking silly with its front wheel a hundred yards away and its nose in a blackened hole, the broken Land-Rover still tied on its back. Luckily, at that moment down the road came trundling one of the oil company's Scammels, a monstrous leviathan of a truck with about two dozen wheels and winches all over the place. This was too good an opportunity to slip. The three-tonner, still with its pickaback Land-Rover, was winched up on to the back of the Scammel, and once again we bade it adieu. A short while later there was a bang . . . the Scammel, however, could lose a wheel or two and not notice it; it merely hiccupped and carried on. Another famous vehicle had the distinction of being blown up twice in one afternoon. The first time was legitimate, and the second came when it was being towed into camp—the towing vehicle missed the mine but the wretched casualty bought it again.

The layers of these menaces numbered about three, at that stage. Originally brother Talib had laid all the mines himself, but he had passed on the secret to a selected few. They would sling a sack of mines over their shoulder, amble down from the mountain-top, and spend a week or two with friends in one of the villages around us—Mutti or Izki or Balad Sait—strolling out each night to plant one of their stock. When it was exhausted they climbed up again for more. These small intervals gave us a breathing space in what was otherwise almost non-stop disaster.

The primitive tactics, and the exiguous numbers of operators, were only revealed after the end of the campaign. In those days we were groping in the dark. A man by the name of Al Qasayer—meaning "Shorty"—was, we were told, responsible; it was also he who did all the shooting at night. But Al Qasayer never materialized except as a disembodied name, and we became increasingly inclined to suspect anybody at all who was not wearing the Sultan's cap badge, and to regard the entire population of Oman with suspicion and even loathing.

We tried every imaginable counter-measure. We sent out nocturnal patrols in almost embarrassing quantities, but a slinking mountaineer could always keep out of the way of a posse of soldiers in that open broken country. We conscripted the villagers—especially those of Mutti and Izki—into rustic picquets, on the principle of setting thieves to catch a thief. All this achieved was the concentration of the mines in stretches of the road where the picquet came from a tribe other than Suleiman's or the Imam's. We obtained a number of mine detectors from the British Army; but it takes a trained expert ten minutes to clear a hundred yards of road, and we had some two hundred miles to cope with. When an important convoy was due we adopted desperate suicide tactics, sending heavily sand-bagged trucks of our own ahead to lay down their lives for their friends. We even considered tarmacadaming the entire stretch, but the cost worked out at more than several hundred lorries, so we abandoned that idea.

Our most fantastic idea of all was inspired by the D-day landings. We dreamt up a flail, like the flail tank, to lumber in front of the convoys bashing the ground and setting off any mines in its path. Surprisingly, the invention was taken up by the usually sceptical oil company, who produced a mine-beating behemoth in their Fahud workshops. They took a gigantic bulldozer and welded on to its side a small bulldozer. They took off the dozer blade and replaced it with a rotating drum to which they had welded a number of heavy chains with iron balls on the end. The big tractor provided mobility, and the small one drove the flail.

The great day came; the elephantine contraption arrived at Izki for field trials, complete with a bashful-looking driver. We planted a captured mine in its path, stood back with our hands over our ears, and watched while the thrashing juggernaut thundered forward.

Nothing happened. The thing reversed, tried again; then again. On its fourth try there was a bright flash and a loud bang, and the end of one of the chains—ball and all—buzzed close over our heads. It worked : but a mine-beater which only worked on the third or fourth run was a poor protection to the convoy travelling trustingly behind it. We thanked the oil company for their generosity, and their ingenuity, and as far as I know the flail is still rusting peacefully at Izki where it rested immovable after its heroic effort.

In those days we could afford to be fairly philosophical about the mines, apart from the fatigue of recovering and backloading their victims, because they were of a small type which was no great menace to human life or limb. A man in a Land-Rover sitting immediately over the explosion suffered a broken ankle, until we took to sand-bagging the scuttles; in a three-tonner the driver was safe from injury, and the vehicle was always repairable. In time we even brought in armour plating for the Land-Rovers, dispensing with the awkward sand-bags. But in time, too, the rebels got a supply of heavier mines—probably first introduced by that horrible lorry from Sharjah—and we had to provide armour plate for the trucks as well, and make sure that our Land-Rovers travelled at the rear.

We never defeated the mines. They remained a constant companion of our daily lives, and a potent inducement to get up that mountain and clear the top of it of mines and men—as soon as we were strong enough, and the weather cooled down.

Mines were not our only worry. One day Anderson and I were sitting enjoying our breakfast—Rognons aux Champignons or something—when a splutter of distant musketry raised our eyebrows. Shortly afterwards a lorry slid to a panic-struck stop at the gate and a dusty and wide-eyed driver cried out that a convoy from Nizwa had been ambushed five miles up the road and was pinned down and being steadily shot to pieces—unable to move—escort running out of ammunition—all the vehicles immobilized—he had been tail-end truck and had managed to escape.

This was new. For the first time for many months the rebels had come down to challenge us by daylight. Nor was it any hit-and-run raid : the spasmodic gunfire was still crackling on.

I swallowed the last of my rognons and pulled a couple of sections and a mortar detachment out of their tents and drove off to see what I could do.

We came to a place where the road went over a dip and round a bare brown spur of the mountain. From just round the corner out of sight I could hear the sporadic crack of shot and a despairing trickle of Bren gun fire in reply. Even more alarming, out of the palm groves and mud tenements of Izki village nearby came piling a wolfish pack of armed Arabs, led by a white-turbaned man in dark glasses which made him look more like a Russian spy in fancy dress than anything else. However, he revealed himself as the Sultan's governor in Izki, and his piratical companions as his gendarmerie. If I needed any help, he told me, I had only to ask. The wild array settled themselves con-

101

spicuously on top of a convenient ridge to pick their noses and
watch the battle.

As soon as I poked my head round the spur and over the dip
I could see that the convoy was at its last gasp. It sprawled
brokenly all over an exposed plain, abjectly at the mercy of the
sharp-shooters on the spur who maintained a regular round-a-
minute to show that they were still there—they were on top of
the salient, facing the other side, and owing to the slope of the
hill I and my relieving column were out of sight and out of the
line of fire. But the convoy was an Aunt Sally. Lorries lay about,
tyres punctured and bodies perforated, and every minute or so
another hole appeared in a bonnet or cab. Huddled miserably
against the wheels on the lee side were little groups of soldiers,
trying to make themselves as tiny as they could, while here and
there a man with a reserve of courage or of ammunition poked a
gun round the edge of his cover and jabbed off a few blind shots
at the stony hill.

The first thing I did was mad. With the mortar on the back
of my Land-Rover I drove over the dip and round the spur
straight into the target zone and told the wide-eyed sergeant to
set it up and start to make noises. A volley of accurate shots
spattered between our legs and sent us scuttling for the cover of
a nearby hillock, where we tried again. Here it was cooler, and
soon enough black and brown puffs from the top of the spur
showed that our bombs were falling in about the right place.
The sniping ceased.

I tried to organize a blanket of covering fire while one of the
infantry sections scrambled up the slope, but the Bren-gunner
was new to the job and endangering our own side, so I took it
from him and began to squeeze off the regulation bursts at the
spur while the section clambered gingerly up the side. By the
time they reached the top the ambush had retreated to a knoll
higher up, and we contented ourselves with lobbing mortar
bombs in their general direction to keep them out of range while
mechanics and spare tyres came hurrying up from Anderson.
The convoy was rescued at last; the snipers grew tired of the
game and disappeared up their Jebel to home, and we withdrew
to ours.

This happened more than once, and the dip and spur earned the name of Windy Corner. It was the only place where the road actually brushed the skirt of the Jebel Akhdhar itself, and it became a favourite shooting gallery for Talib's sportsmen. Soon we had to establish a permanent picquet on top of the spur, which further depleted our reserves of men at Izki; but it rendered the corner less windy, and we could concentrate on the mines again.

In these days Gunpowder Joe, that unusual medical orderly, was part of our team, having—like myself and Bob Warner— left the Trucial Oman Levies to see what life was like in the proper Oman. He was unlucky enough to go over a mine and break both his ankles, and for many weeks he could be seen irrepressibly hopping around in the course of his duties with both legs encased in plaster of Paris. In between patching up shot-wounds and mine injuries he administered his bottled nostrums for constipation and gonorrhea, he extracted teeth, and generally maintained morale.

The long-awaited secret weapon was unleashed on Izki in the middle of the year. We laughed at Talib's riflemen, after we had finished our wall, but his new 81-mm mortars—in theory— could overleap the highest ramparts. His men tried very hard. They dared not set up a permanent mortar post, for fear of what we would do to it if they did, so they had to keep the things tucked away in crevices in the Jebel and move them out and put them up afresh every time they wanted to shoot at us. This is no way to serve a mortar : it is accurate only after careful laying and ranging. Nevertheless, at the height of their bombardments they lugged the clumsy thing out every evening just at dusk, to the entrance of a ravine which faced Izki camp about two miles distant. They then loosed off a desperate salvo before our own mortars, which were aimed with great precision on the mouth of the gorge, could respond. They sent us a half dozen rounds or so, then hurriedly ducked back inside the ravine while our own weapons retaliated. This game went on for some time, but only once did Talib's bombardiers manage to lob one inside our wall—luckily for us, because that one did serious damage, material and human, in the narrow confines of the camp. But nor did we ever hit their mortars. It was a duel without a victory. What they never discovered was that their 81-mm mortar could out-range our old-fashioned 3-inch machine; if they had set theirs up just out of our range they could have hammered away in peace.

Gradually the build-up on the mountain was having its effect. Big mines, which caused death or grievous injury; mortars; heavy machine-guns, which silenced our aeroplane equipped with loudspeakers to blare loyal exhortations over the whole green plateau (it had to jettison its mouthpieces and limp home dumb); a more professional, less shag-haired personnel in the enemy picquets and ambushes—all told the same tale. The dreadful trio were growing stronger every day.

But so were we.

The Sultan in those days had a small piece of Asia which he called his own. This was the town of Gwadur, on the coast at the extreme Persian end of West Pakistan. The inhabitants were Baluchis, a sort of hybrid Iranian race, whose fealty to His Highness of Muscat derived from a quirk of history. From Gwadur came a regular flow of recruits to the Sultan's army. The Sultan sagely decided that there was small point in trying to recruit his own tribesmen, when most of them were either revolting or teetering on the edge of revolt. It was certain that if the Imam's rebellion succeeded almost every tribe in the country would follow the white flag, and no tribe at that time was prepared to risk the mistake of choosing the wrong colour.

So the Baluchis came to Muscat, in shiploads. The Baluchi is a cheerful soul of placid humour and no imagination : this makes him a staunch soldier under stress, but hard to inspire to heroic exertions. In all this he is the complete antithesis of the Arab. He has, moreover, one major disadvantage. He only speaks Baluchi, a language known only to Baluchis. It is most difficult to lead soldiers if they speak a private tongue. In a tight corner you have to be able to say, rapidly, "Jones, take your Bren and a couple of men to the top of that ridge—the one with the flat tree—and as soon as you see us coming up out of that dip down there, fire at the black rock with the big shadow on it—yes, that's the one—until we are down in the next gully." And having said it, you must be sure that you are understood. It was hard enough with Arab soldiers—we all spoke Arabic, but few of us spoke it as fluently as that: but how to command troops whose language was not even recognized by the London School of Oriental Studies?

While I was on leave for a couple of months in London I tried to do something about this problem. I approached the London School, who implied that they knew of no such tongue. I tramped the streets of Bloomsbury, trying all the more obscure bookshops. At last I found a more than usually erudite shop—appropriately enough, just opposite the British Museum—and went in and asked if they had so strange a thing as a book on the Baluchi language.

An old and scholarly-looking man said yes, he thought they had had one somewhere—some time . . . he climbed upstairs and rummaged, and after a while he tottered down again bearing in his arms a mildewed cardboard box, one corner of which had been consumed by mice. It was, apart from these nibblings, untouched. He opened it, and there lay four dozen dark red volumes in mint condition, fresh from the publishers, immaculate but for a few gnawed corners, odorous with some long-dead printer's ink. The book had been published in the 1880s, and presumably had never been heard of since, except by this ancient curator. It was called *A Grammar of the Baloochee Language*, and its chapters were headed "Of Nouns", "Of the Verb", and so on : a collector's piece.

I bought half a dozen of these precious volumes, which had after all some strategic significance in the outlandish campaign of Oman, and I took them back with me to Muscat where they proved invaluable. At last we could communicate with our soldiers.

As well as our Baluchis, we were getting more and more help from the British Army. I have already mentioned the magnificent Marines, who trained our men—even the Baluchis, using the universal language of the drill square—and led patrols and generally distinguished themselves, with, so far as I know, very little public recognition considering it was not their war. We had a company of Trucial Oman Scouts, by now permanently stationed at Izki to share with our own company there the threefold burden of defending ourselves, escorting convoys, and policing the countryside; and we had a detachment of armoured cars, whose enormous advantage was that they could get in close to the enemy and shoot at them without much danger.

And one day we got some big guns.

We still had our small guns, but they were too tiny to do what we were aching to do in these months: thump the top of the Jebel Akhdhar. So the British Government kindly presented His Highness with two pieces of medium artillery, of five-and-a-half-inch bore, big enough to need special heavy tractors to tow them (our own little toys could be put on the back of a Land-Rover). A Royal Artillery officer came to us to show us how to work them, and he soon trained a troop of burly Baluchis in big black boots who tossed the great shells around as though they were tennis balls.

We could not hit Sharaija from Nizwa, so we had to take the guns out to a site near the foot of the mountain. It was not long before our splendid ordnance was banging away, cocked up at howitzer angles, flinging up high explosive over into the very heart of Suleiman's kingdom.

Nor was it long before Talib reacted, angrily. One day the artillery convoy lumbering to its playground came under heavy fire from the surrounding hills; the giant tractors went up on mines; and the whole enterprise developed into a daily small war before the guns could begin their work in peace. John Clarke, that midnight mountaineer, commanded the home company at Nizwa, and it was his job every day to go out ahead of the guns and clear the area. This became more and more of a labour— "a battle a day", said he with dismal enthusiasm—and shortly yet another of our three companies was tied down securely, as at Izki, in a defensive task, in this case on permanent sentry-go for the gun-site. We built a camp of palm thatch, dug holes all round it for soldiers to hide in, posted picquets among the rocks on dominating hills, draped barbed wire elegantly around, made kitchens, cleared paths—for the sole purpose of protecting our two precious guns, whose detonations in our midst smashed regularly our nightly sleep.

Slowly but irretrievably the whole army was getting bogged down. The bangs of our guns were the only sign that we were doing anything at all to discomfit the Imam on his elevated throne.

Somebody had another bright idea. Why not booby-trap the exits from the Jebel? As there were so few ways up, so there were correspondingly few ways down. If we were getting blown up because we were obliged to use the roads, surely the rebels could be equally blown up because they were confined to certain tracks in and out of their mountain keep.

There were difficulties. The mouths of the ravines were all a clutter of large boulders, some as big as a house, so anti-personnel mines were out. Also, for every man who came and went, perhaps two dozen goats and half a hundred rabbits, foxes, and hedge-hogs used the same right of way. So a technical expert from the Royal Engineers was lent to us (the British Army was becoming more and more helpful, offering us most things short of actual soldiers, which it had sworn never to send to Oman again). This ingenious sapper concocted a sort of fougasse out of a 3-inch mortar bomb, fixed to a trip wire so that small game could pass underneath unscathed but a man would trigger the thing and demolish himself. A goat would do the same; but no loyal goat had any business going up the Jebel, and Talib's goats deserved all they would get.

This sapper was a dauntless man of inexhaustible energy. He laid every single booby trap himself, which meant penetrating into one after another of the gloomy gorges and staying there long enough to set his gins. Daily he strode off towards the mountains, stripped to the buff, brown as a nut, with a clumsy army haversack over his gleaming shoulder stuffed with high explosives. He was assisted in this chore by a young volunteer from the Artillery name Robertson, who was noted among us as much for his keenness and daring as for his horse-like neigh of a laugh, which used to rouse the whole camp in alarm until we got used to it. Robertson was a real soldier, one of a growing number of young men fed up with Aldershot manœuvres and boot-polishing parades who looked around for the nearest war and found themselves on loan to the Sultan.

Sadly, the booby traps were not a decisive success. The only one I know that was set off by human agency was behind Izki, where a small patrol had been probing gingerly inside the bugged ravine. The men had all been told where the contraption was, but on the way out one of them forgot, and he trod on the trip wire. There was a shattering crash, right in the middle of the patrol, as the mortar bomb obediently exploded; but the only damage was an elbow bruised by a flying pebble.

I think however that this was more the fault of the British mortar bomb than of the sapper's skill. I have a horribly clear recollection of lobbing one of them right into the midst of some of my own men—a bull's eye on the wrong target. But instead of disintegrated limbs and scattered entrails, all I got was raised fists shaken at me and sarcastic comments on my marksmanship from my indignant soldiers—none of them had so much as a scratch. We tried, whenever we could, to use the white phosphorus smoke bomb rather than the H.E.; the shower of inextinguishable phosphorus fire was far more maiming on those mountain slopes than a few pieces of iron fragments and a pebble or two.

Our increasingly ingenious defensive measures, and our reliance on artillery to do our fighting for us on the top of the Jebel, induced a reaction in the breasts of those who came to help us. Being professional members of a proud service, unlike ourselves who were merely mercenaries, some individual Trucial Oman officers, Royal Marines, and others set out during the furnace heat of that heart-breaking summer to show us how we should be tackling Talib. The results were often useful but sometimes tragic.

Mutti was the scene of at least two disasters, impelled by this urge to do something against that grim mountain whose impregnability we of the Sultan's army seemed to have taken for granted, but doomed by ignorance of what that mountain was like. At least, we knew that.

Life in a Hole

Mutti was a village plastered on to the slopes of a ridge of brown rock which lay like a barrier across the mouth of one of the chasms leading to the Jebel plateau. The ravine cutting down behind this ridge turned at right angles to run along its rear, then debouched on to the plains through a cleft with walls going up almost a thousand feet. Mutti had been built to guard this gateway. Towers and turrets paced all along its ridge-back, and a fortified cluster of buildings squatted on the toe of the ridge where it overlooked the emerging ravine. Spread like a blanket below the village was a thick complex of date groves and terraced fields, which could only be negotiated on foot, in single file, and with difficulty. The only legitimate way into Mutti, and the only way vehicles could get anywhere near it, was to drive to the mouth of the gorge and then walk in through the fortified barbican on the point.

Mutti was garrisoned by a gaggle of Tariq's tribal followers, captained by a man named Nasser who had hands like wet fish and a face to match: he was, furthermore, Suleiman bin Himyar's father-in-law. So he was not notably effective in keeping Mutti clear of rebels, many of whom had their homes there and used to spend the weekend with their families.

We at Izki regarded Mutti with great distaste. We used to go there sometimes, to pay official courtesy calls on the clammy Nasser, but with so much else on our hands we were not disposed to provoke any more trouble than necessary: we respected Mutti's titular neutrality, nodded at Nasser's protestations of loyalty, and otherwise kept clear of the place.

This was not good enough for the Trucial Oman Scouts, who saw Mutti—rightly—as a standing insult. One day they marched into the mouth of the ravine in strength, as though with bands playing and colours flying, and were promptly assailed by a hurricane of shot from both sides—they had walked straight into a soldier's nightmare, a perfect ambush with no escape. They were pinned down among the rocks of the gorge, unable to move so much as a finger, for the marksmen on the cliffs above them had perfect command of the whole area. The Company Commander was killed almost at once.

It took one of the biggest battles of the whole campaign to get the Scouts out of that death-trap. Aeroplanes summoned from Sharjah plastered the hillsides with rockets and cannon shells; scout cars, secure in their armour plate, got to grips with the rock walls; all the troops we could spare were thrown into the fray. Mutti was not to be touched with impunity.

Incredibly, almost the same thing happened again within months, this time by mistake. A newly arrived Marine sergeant was doing some routine patrolling with a handful of our men, and thought that he would like to see what was inside that intriguing ravine . . . at least that is what we assumed he must have thought. The sergeant was killed, two of his men wounded, and the rest hopelessly pinned like butterflies to the bare grey rocks. It took most of the day and a great deal of shooting before they could be prised out. After that we installed a permanent garrison of soldiers in Mutti, in the fortified hamlet on the toe of the ridge, to protect our access to Nasser. We poked a few patrols into the gorge from there—one of them set off our booby trap—but Mutti was never properly cleansed, and it remained a sore thumb to the end.

One evening I was driving peacefully along in my Land-Rover to visit a patrol when the whole vehicle suddenly bucked like a broncho, a numbing detonation filled the air with choking dust and black smoke, and I found myself on the ground with my face in a small thorn-bush. It was a moment or two before the smoke thinned and my mind shook itself clear—there was my Land-Rover, with its front blown off; lying around it were my two or three soldiers, white with dust, rigid but unhurt.

My reaction was rage—they'd blown *me* up!—and my own vehicle was a heap of scrap. But thanks to the sand-bags nobody was more than scratched. We hailed a passing cameleer, requisitioned his mount, and one of my escort cantered back to Izki for succour. After some hours, which we spent huddled anxiously behind a protective boulder—we were quite alone, and the Jebel here rose steeply from the roadside—a lorry came from Anderson and hauled us ignominiously home.

That was the end of my first year as a mercenary. I went home on leave, heartily glad of the break.

10

PROFESSIONAL KILLERS TO THE RESCUE

E v e r since the withdrawal of British aid after the recapture of Nizwa in 1957, the Sultan's army had born the brunt of Talib's truculence, with the help for part of the time of a company of Carter's Scouts, the Marine N.C.O.s, and every now and again the bombs of the R.A.F. Our army of occupation consisted of only three companies of Sultan's Baluch, which should have been about ninety strong but never were. Under the command of Colin Maxwell, John Clarke and myself captained two of the companies and a native officer managed the third. We had Jasper and his donkeys, Bob Warner and his stores, Richard Anderson and his Izki camp; there was a dedicated artist with the mortars called Eric Roe, and an intelligence officer named Dennison who had been wounded by one of Saleh bin Issa's friends two years before and still limped on a strapped-up leg. At Bait-al-Falaj, the steamy headquarters near Muscat, flourished Chief of Staff Waterfield—large of frame and imperturbable—and Haugh, late of Haughcol; nearby Pat Gray was still methodically churning out Baluch recruits at the Depot. There was a succession of auxiliaries—the gunner who taught us to fire the guns, the specialist in psychological warfare who tried to persuade the trinity on the mountain to surrender—until his aeroplane had its loudspeakers shot off; there were the steel-clad scout cars. And that, for many months, was our lot.

But our desperate shortage was of ordinary soldiers, and in particular of ordinary officers, and of experienced generalship.

Maxwell had held the line splendidly but it was giving way all round, the three little companies were tied hard down protecting their own homes and their own lines of communication, and there was now no hope at all of doing what obviously had to be done—climbing up that awful mountain with enough men to capture it. Bombs and booby traps would never put an end to our woes, which grew more woeful with every day that passed.

So the British Army generously took us over.

This brought about a revolution in our ranks. We were overwhelmed by officers—we were very grateful for them, too. Maxwell went to Muscat and a shiny lieutenant-colonel assumed command of the troops at Nizwa and Izki, who were glorified by the name of Northern Frontier Regiment (notwithstanding the fact that they were stationed plumb in the middle of the country, and the nearest frontier was the desert to the west). Another lieutenant-colonel, Mike Read, came to command the soldiers at Bait-al-Falaj who were called—more reasonably—the Muscat Regiment. These colonels came trailing a cloud of junior officers, who quickly and enthusiastically set out to show us what they could do. Some of them were first class, and one in particular, John Churchill, won the Military Cross with us.

And on top of the lot came Colonel David Smiley, to take command of all the Sultan's forces. Previous to this, the commander had been nominally His Highness himself, and the operative overlord was the sagacious Waterfield who called himself Chief of Staff after the British pattern. But although we mercenaries were happy enough under this arrangement, the newcomers were not, because they needed to have their own "commander" for reasons connected with the Army Act and oaths of allegiance. The Sultan and his Chief of Staff could not exercise legal authority over them. So Smiley assumed the title of "Commander". Waterfield, not to be outdone, thereupon transformed himself into Military Secretary, a tailor-made office which was a sort of Minister of Defence and bore the rank of brigadier. Watching this escalation from the lower rungs, we expected to see the Secretaryship evolve as a mere formality, and that Waterfield's position would henceforth be a rich bowler-hatted sinecure in recompense for past services. But we reckoned

112

without our Waterfield. Released from the immediate cares of military minutiae, he grew—almost physically, it seemed to us—and rose, a balloon of authority, until he floated like an exalted potentate over all Muscat and Oman. In a word, he remained on top. We thought that if we had been Smiley we would have made ourselves at least a brigadier too, if not a major-general, but he withstood the temptation.

David Smiley was an exceptional man. He was short, with unblinking eyes and a flat mild face like a parson. He was as tough as teak. In his time he had jingled down the Mall in charge of the Sovereign's Escort of Royal Horse Guards—complete with breast-plate and horse-feather helmet, which we found hard to envisage. During the war he had jumped into the Balkans and organized Yugoslav partisans under the eyes of the Germans. He had friends in the most lofty places, an unslakable thirst for danger, and a tall beautiful wife. Whoever chose him for us was a genius, for Smiley's combination of guerilla pugnacity and Guards punctilio was really what we had all been needing for a long time.

After the take-over we at last stepped into proper uniform. Before this we had dressed in more or less what we liked—or, as in the primordial Trucial Oman Levies, whatever we had left. Jasper wore his revolting khaki hat, I had an even more disgusting once-blue beret, others swished around in Lawrence of Arabia head-dress like the Scouts. Colin Maxwell sported a balmoral, a memento of his service in the Royal Scots Fusiliers, and this pom-pommed pancake caught the Sultan's eye one day when the new uniforms were being designed. "Like that," decreed His Highness, pointing at Maxwell's khaki bonnet—"but in scarlet."

So the Muscat Regiment, including the unfortunate Mike Read, an elderly officer of great charm and quiet proficiency—were all decked out in bright red balmorals. What the Edinburgh bonnet-makers thought of this strange command from an Arabian Sultan has not been recorded, but they fulfilled the order without audible demur. The Muscat Regiment, not being Scots, never learnt to put the things on properly, and they looked more like a parade of scarlet toadstools than military men. One of their new officers was, however, a Scot, and he tried to show the Arabs, Baluchis, and Sassenachs of the Regiment how to wear their new hats, but it was no use. Richard Anderson by this time had joined the Muscat Regiment and with his globular shape and flat red headgear he resembled a rissole with a slice of tomato on top.

The Northern Frontier Regiment were spared this indignity, and continued to use their green berets; this outraged the Commandos, but the Sultan could do what he liked with his own army. Headquarters, including David Smiley, wore scarlet berets like Egyptian policemen. Brigadier Waterfield wore what he liked.

All these infusions of new blood and boatloads of funny hats could still not win us the Jebel Akhdhar. Nevertheless, it had to be won during the coming winter, whatever the cost—none of us could bear to contemplate another year like the one we had just been through.

The lessons we had learnt were however taken to heart by our new masters. There were no more mad patrols, no more waterless walks up the defended passes, no more traps for us to bait and the R.A.F. to spring with bombs; and no more suicidal onslaughts into the mouth of Mutti gorge.

By November 1958 Smiley had mobilized all his immense influence with principalities and powers. He intercepted a company of Special Air Service who were on their way home from warring in the Malayan jungles, and persuaded them to break their journey to do a small job for us. . . .

The S.A.S. were airborne commandos, possessing the qualities and faculties of both commandos and paratroops. They were the coolest and most frightening body of professional killers I have ever seen—the ordinary Commandos were perfect gentlemen in comparison. A company of these battle-hardened toughs was worth a regiment of infantry and probably a division of our staunch but stolid and unintelligible Baluchis.

The S.A.S. were calmly confident. They examined maps, flew recces over the Jebel, and gave it as their opinion that three weeks should suffice for the "job". In the event it took them three months, and they had to double their strength by sending for another company; but they did it.

They tried, first of all, one or two conventional approaches. A patrol scrambled up the ridge on the other side of Mutti gorge from the village, and were promptly pinned down by a handful of rebels who had seen them coming and raced them to the top. It took a long time, and a large barrage of mortar bombs, before they could move at all. They came down again.

They went up in other places, too—but being the fit and sensible soldiers they were, they went up the sides, not the ravines. These flanks, it will be remembered, provided no route to the Jebel because they terminated in pointed peaks looking down on the plateau over vertical or hanging precipices; but the S.A.S. noted all this down in their reports and methodically went on patrolling.

One reconnaissance marched up the other side, from Awabi. They found an unguarded route, like Darwish's from Tanuf, which led them on to the high point which I had reached with Darwish the year before. Sensibly, and gleefully, they determined at once not to relinquish this priceless foothold on the very top of the mountain. Smiley reinforced them and kept them supplied, and they stayed up there. But they were still on the wrong side of that col guarded by its natural gatehouse which I had tried in vain to get the R.A.F. to soften up. Unless they stormed this strongpoint they were no nearer to Sharaija and Talib than we were, on the ground at Izki. They did try to take it, but failed. Clearly, another way had to be found.

But all this offensive activity was affecting the defenders' nerves. The Royal Air Force, too, was becoming even more aggressive. Almost every day now we heard crumps, thumps, and distant drum-rolls where they plastered suspected picquets with bigger and yet bigger bombs. They machine-gunned goats, and generally did everything short of actually bombing Sharaija, which would have been—according to the existing code of behaviour for such occasions—an act of undeclared war. All the time, however, our great guns were banging away at Sharaija, and hitting it more and more often. And the patrols, those of the S.A.S. and those by our own troops, boldly led by our new young

officers, were now forcing Talib to disperse his troops. He knew
the blow was coming, but he was increasingly confused about
where it was coming from, and he had to guard more and more
of the approaches, whereas in our early days he could see us
coming from afar and collect all his strength against us.

The build-up went on remorselessly. Stewart Carter sent us
truck-loads of his Scouts, and then he came down himself to join
the fun. We had some Life Guards in armoured cars: they
climbed out of them and played infantry and ascended to join
the S.A.S. on the mountain peak. The Muscat Regiment got into
the game. Hundreds of tribesmen rallied once more, waving flags
and firing joyous guns. To supply this burgeoning army Smiley
brought three hundred donkeys over from Somaliland, and with
them a professional donkey man of the Army Veterinary Service.
From all sides they came. David Smiley was making sure that
we lacked nothing, human or animal or material, for what had
to be the last and decisive assault on the Imam's castle of rock.

At this interesting juncture I abruptly departed from the stage.
I had a difference of opinion with one of the new colonels, about
what was and was not militarily feasible. He was a lion of a man
but he had at that time no conception of what the Jebel was
like. It was a symptom of the sometimes strained relations between the "old guard"—Maxwell, Jasper and company—and
the new blood, that my disagreements with this gentleman were
taken the wrong way. So I left the battle area and went to the
coast on a new assignment. A slight smell of cowardice came to
hover for a while over my departure, unbeknown to me until
much later; however, this soon evaporated.

It was sad but perhaps unavoidable, that some suspicion and
disharmony should develop between the two elements in our
army: the Sultan's regulars and the British Army annexures.
We were conscious that we had had to be bailed out of trouble;
we were touchy, quick to detect a slight and to take offence; and
we tended to look for the newcomers sniffing at us. They in their
turn must have felt the subterranean resentment. They disliked
our cliquishness, our assumption of knowing best, our air of having been there from the beginning when things were bad. Some

of them were in fact pretty offensive, and even insubordinate, but these were few, and they were in any case the less distinguished element. Two men who fought long and hard, and in the end prevailed against this schism, were Smiley himself, and Colin Maxwell, who was Smiley's Deputy Commander and exerted great tact upon the sniffers on both sides.

Whatever the motives were, I was made an example. I handed over my men, most of whom had been with me for a year and some—especially the native officers and senior N.C.O.s—since Haughcol. I gave them into good hands, the neighing Robertson and John Churchill who was to win the M.C. with them, and I departed for my new parish.

The Batina Coast of Oman ran all the way up from Muscat to the root of the rhinoceros's horn. It was a dull plain, ranging in width from twenty miles to nothing, and its entire length of two hundred miles was virtually one long village. Lining the beach the whole way, perched precariously on sand dunes, was a continuous succession of fishing villages built of the universal palm thatch and decorated with drying fish and nets. At regular thirty-mile intervals there was a town, with market and mosque and a crumbling castle in which sat a Sultan's Governor dispensing justice and collecting bribes. Backing the sand dunes and fishermen's huts was a ribbon of salt marsh planted with date palms. At the back of these was another series of villages and castles, devoted mostly to the raising of goats, and clusters of brushwood hovels among the bushes inhabited by shepherds and their flocks. The entire inhabited strip was about five miles broad. Inland of the goat belt an expanse of grey gravel desert stretched to the foothills of the Jebel Akhdar.

Travel up and down the Batina was always tedious and often excruciating. Living there engendered a one-dimensional view of life : there were only two directions to go, left or right, up or down the coast. There were four parallel roads. For the bold, the impatient, or the knowledgeable, there was the beach at low tide, where a truck could hum along at a steady sixty miles an hour—but exits were few and wide apart, and a miscalculation of tide or a breakdown meant a salt-water bath for the vehicle. The less adventurous could grind along the tops of the sand dunes, wind serpentine through palm groves, or churn up a choking cloud of dust on the inland route. Most of us varied the anguish by hopping from one to the other. When it rained there was no choice : the low-lying palm groves became a waterlogged swamp, the powdery inland dust changed to melted chocolate, and the only way was over the switchback sand dunes, with here and there a detour through somebody's back garden when a gully washed across the path.

This merciless journey could take two days, and never less than a full day, except by trusting Poseidon and charging along the beach. Even then there were hazards, most numerous early in the morning, when whole villages were evacuating their bowels on the foreshore. Rounding a point at 60 m.p.h. full tilt into two dozen defecating fishermen is an unnerving experience.

The capital of the Batina is Sohar, an interesting town of some antiquity. From Sohar, we are told, Sinbad the Sailor took to sea. At Sohar I set up house in one of the Sultan's holiday villas, a two-storey damp-floored house with red Mangalore tiles, a garden of coconuts, guavas, and okra, a charcoal kitchen, an Indian cook, string beds and an Elsan bucket.

My job on the Batina was to stop arms and men coming in to reinforce Talib while Smiley was getting into his stride. Two hundred miles of open coastline to watch, with apparently nobody to do it but myself, seemed an exacting task. I drove for two whole days through a rainstorm to the utmost border, a customs post in the hills guarding the road to Sharjah and Dubai. There, in a palm-leaf hut, sipping his private whisky out of a tin mug, was Jasper.

Jasper had preceded me out of the Northern Frontier Regiment : perhaps he had been an earlier victim of the purge. A retired group captain cannot make the easiest subordinate to a temporary lieutenant-colonel. Jasper did his damnedest to be a junior officer but sometimes his group captaincy burst through despite himself, especially when provoked by gross stupidity. Jasper, I found, had been camped at the customs post for some weeks, trying to locate a consignment of rifles which somebody had said were on their way through for Talib. With him was a second half-brother of the Sultan, a courtly gentleman named Fahar, who, like Tariq in the interior, was a sort of overlord of the Batina. Fahar was stout and zealous but he lacked Tariq's force of character and he was a bit of a trial for the Governors and customs men he was supposed to supervise; but he was useful and energetic and pleasant company, and, as the only person within two hundred miles who could speak English, he probably kept me sane.

Jasper had with him his donkey, and he had collected a miscellany of exiled Persian smugglers from whom he was improbably composing an *ad hoc* gendarmerie. These extraordinary people were the followers of an Iranian chieftain who had rebelled against the Shah and fled for asylum to Oman, where they had settled and built up a considerable living for themselves by smuggling, slaving, and gun-running. They were, therefore, ideal for this job : smugglers set to catch smugglers. They knew all the routes, they knew the agents and the cameleers and the corruptible customs officers; they were, moreover, indubitably loyal to the Sultan, who had given them a home, and they nursed a deep dislike of the native Omani Arabs which was cordially returned.

So Jasper had rounded up these gentlemen, had armed them, organized them into sections and platoons, appointed corporals and sergeants and disposed them in the hills astride the border where they could intercept improper traffic. The very day I arrived they bagged a respected local sheikh on his way home from a shopping spree in Sharjah who was taking a short cut home, which happened by chance to avoid the customs post.

The heirs to the rebellious chieftain were two youngish men of startling flamboyance called Mirza and Jan Mohammed. Mirza, the elder, was tall and handsome and theatrically grand. When he spoke it was as one possessed of ancestral wisdom and priestly knowledge; every movement and gesture was a study in grave significance; he was soft-spoken, darkly dressed, and inscrutable. Jan Mohammed was like Errol Flynn. He had sweeping black mustachios and flashing eyes and teeth. He dressed himself up like a film sheikh, white robes, flowing headgear and crossed bandoliers and three or four guns and pistols stuck into belts. He seemed to swoop, eagle-like, rather than to walk, and his speech was all a dazzle of ivory and braggadocio. He was on the whole less impressive than Mirza—he lacked Mirza's calculated portentousness. But he was the finer spectacle.

These characters were appointed honorary lieutenants by Jasper and they amicably divided the command and the spoils between themselves. They, and some two or three dozen of their fellows, were the nucleus of my new command.

Jasper had by now finished his mug of whisky; he saddled his long-eared steed, and took himself off to the Jebel where he charged up and down at the head of another tribal levy.

I sat down in his palm-leaf hut and contemplated my assignment with growing consternation.

There was a daunting number of things to be done, which Jasper had had time only to begin. The legendary consignment of rifles had to be found, intercepted, or refuted. The Persian buccaneers had to be mustered, exhorted, and generally worked into some kind of recognizable shape as an instrument of law and order. The entire frontier should be explored, to survey the clandestine routes through the hills. Customs men, provincial governors, and village notables had to be sought, interviewed, cultivated, and if possible poised eagerly on their toes. To most of them the natural position was a squat on the buttocks, to which they returned when released, like coiled springs. The whole coast line had to be patrolled, as often as possible, and Mirza's freebooters disseminated along it, with instructions to apprehend smugglers of arms and men.

But the most important task of all, of which the overriding urgency had never yet been faced, was intelligence : to develop a system of eyes and ears so that never again would we be caught as we had been by Talib in 1957, by Saleh bin Issa's truck in 1958; so that we could stem the apparently unceasing flow of mines; so that we could know, among the indistinguishable multitudes of smiling and scowling bearded faces, who were our friends and who our real enemies.

We had been far too busy since the outbreak of revolt to spare men, time, or energy to do this. Malcolm Dennison, with his strapped-up leg, had looked after it for a time and had begun to strike roots, but he threw away his crutches one day and became a company commander. Thenceforward we had negligible contact with the underworld. Waterfield at Bait-al-Falaj enjoyed access to the Sultan's own secret bureau, but this produced little of any immediate use and a surprising amount of pure fiction. Our own efforts, through personal contact with Governors and chiefs, were futile; those—a rapidly decreasing number—who were still genuinely disposed to help us, either knew nothing or merely picked up and passed on a garbled mess of sensational rumours. Those in the know were not our friends.

Talib was observed, generally disguised as a woman, almost every day, and dutifully reported to us, in places often scores of miles apart. We had long ago given up looking for him, and one of the hundred rumours was eventually found to have been true. The rebels on the mountain were hourly expected to throw in the sponge and creep submissively down from Sharaija—we even had to call off one fighting patrol for fear of frightening a quite imaginary emissary of peace. We were led to believe that Talib had furnished himself with unlimited supplies of even more alarming weapons than he really had—bazookas, even anti-tank guns, which gave our scout-car crews some anxious moments. We spent a lot of time and petrol chasing a supply convoy from Saudi Arabia which was supposed to be delivering weapons and ammunition straight across the Empty Quarter. This turned out to be harmless bedouin carting blocks of rock salt from a dry lake in the far west. Nizwa received regular reports that a party of men would come at such and such a time of night, by such and such a road, to shoot at the camp. They used to send out ambushes, for a while, but soon gave it up : men did come and shoot at the camp, but never when expected, nor by the forecast route.

And the most persistent and extravagant rumours were beginning to adhere to certain names, which sounded over and over again until they assumed the proportions of mythological heroes. There was Al Qasayer, the sinister Shorty, who was credited personally with every mine and every round of ammunition fired at Izki. Did he exist, we wondered? Or was he a sort of composite creature, an allegorical scapegoat, an elaborate smoke-screen? It was a long time before we discovered the truth about Al Qasayer; but we began to suspect that he was more than one person, and the number of times we were told that we had killed him, or he blew himself up on one of our mortar-bomb booby-traps or one of his own mines, suggested a whole tribe of subversive short men.

The desperate thing was that we simply did not know. We were better informed than in 1957 : we had found out, through a great deal of hard and often dangerous work, what the Green Mountain was really like—we had come a long way from the days when we used to sit around a hurricane lamp and read the old explorer's archaic prose to each other. But we knew the name of scarcely one of the men opposing us, except the three leaders and Al Qasayer; we never knew where any of the leaders were, so that we might bomb or shell their hideout; and we never knew, in all the land of Oman, who could be trusted and who was a subcutaneous agent of the Imam. We ran around in circles chasing reports and rumours, seeking caches of mines, searching for knots of rebels. And none of it was true.

The same sad situation prevailed on the Batina. Apart from what Fahar might have known, and whatever professional know-ledge was stored in the heads of the gendarmes, I—and Jasper before me—laboured in the dark. But Fahar, for all his loyalty, had little idea of what constituted useful intelligence and what was merely interesting gossip; and the smugglers were wise enough to keep their trade secrets securely locked up under their turbans.

It seemed hopeless. I needed either a thousand incorruptible police, or a reliable ear to the ground. I had neither; but the second seemed more realistic a requirement.

I drove like a yoyo up and down the coast, sometimes suffocat-ing in dust and sometimes slavered in mud. I sought the reluctant confidence of sheikhs, of merchants, of busybodies. After many days I achieved a measure of rapport with Mirza and Jan Mohammed, by travelling interminably with them and spending gossipy nights in their leaf-mat house and sharing their delicious Persian meals—rich spiced chicken and lacy wafery bread; until they offered to introduce me to one or two friends of theirs who might—just might—be able to help me. I had been issued with a small supply of money for use on such an opportunity, and I visited these men. One was a moth-eaten major domo in the house of a sheikh known to be an active enemy of the Sultan but too powerful to be locked up. This bedraggled butler was affable but uninformative, he took his crumpled banknote and vowed to get in touch with me directly he overheard any indiscretions at his master's table. I never saw him again. Another was a sharp young man who ran a taxi business, one who could be expected to know peculiar people and to take in a large daily ration of gossip. He pocketed my money with profuse promises, and that was the last I saw of him.

My third introduction was even more improbable. He was elderly and indolent, a small farmer in a desultory way and a vaguely part-time merchant—a typical Batina bourgeois. He was of the same Persian tribe as the gendarmes, and he spoke bad Arabic with a heavy accent. He was not at all the kind of person who would be privy to the secrets of the Imam. However, I politely made his acquaintance, revealed my purpose by elaborate circumlocution, and pressed my third and last note into his hand. He accepted it graciously, but said he was doubtful that he could be of any use to me. . . .

Some days later I was accosted at the door of my villa in Sohar by a grizzled, smelly, and dishevelled camel-man. I had never seen him before, but he invited himself in, sat down on one of my arm chairs, and told me a tale.

He was connected in some way, he said, to the recipient of my third banknote : related, indebted, indentured or enslaved— I was never quite clear. Following my visit, his patron had despatched him to Sharjah and Dubai, there to act the part of a man having a consignment of mines and to cast around for one willing to help him move them into Oman. I considered this fairy-story an insult to my intelligence—in both senses of the word; but I was careful not to offend him, and he went on with his romance. He had found just such a fellow, he claimed : a taxi driver; he even gave me a name. He recited names of other characters who were in the plot, including a goat-herd near

123

Sohar who was to take over the cargo from the taxi-driver and distribute it. He himself was to return to Sharjah at a predetermined date and confer with his accomplices again, after which he would communicate with me further. There was just one small thing—on his last trip he had tried to bring his own rifle, really his own, through the customs post—quite openly—and the officials there had been unkind enough to impound it. Would I therefore please give him a chit to redeem his rifle?

I was tempted to push him bodily out of the house. I was soft enough, however, to prevaricate. I told him that I would consider his request if he went back to Sharjah and brought us some material evidence on which we could act. He was sadly transparent, I thought; merely trying to smuggle a rifle through customs and trusting to my gullibility—I dismissed him, with a sinking opinion of my own acumen and of the bona fides of Mirza and Jan Mohammed.

Only a few days after this came news that the war was over. The Green Mountain was in the hands of the Sultan. My ragged man came back and said there was now no point in his going to Sharjah and could he have his rifle? I said no; and that seemed the end of my cloak and daggery. I left the Batina and my eccentric job and returned to ordinary peacetime soldiering. Another year passed before I discovered how right he had been, and what a priceless pearl I had thrown away.

The Jebel Akhdhar had been taken by the only way it could have been taken—the impossible way. The S.A.S. walked up the right hand slab alongside the route I had first taken with Jasper a year and a half before. After a glance at the sheer wall dropping down from the apex of the triangle, they calmly knotted ropes and lowered themselves commando-fashion down on to the plateau; and there they were. Talib's picquets were outflanked, and the way to Sharaija was open.

Resistance collapsed at once, as soon as the defenders saw that their fortress, impregnable for a thousand years, had been stormed in so nonchalant a fashion. Soldiers, donkeys, tribesmen swarmed up on all sides.

The war was over.

There was just one minor worry, one small speck on the otherwise triumphant horizon.

Where was Suleiman bin Himyar? Where was Talib?

Where, above all, was the Imam?

11

REVOLTING SOLDIERY

T H E weeks succeeding the victory on the Jebel floated by in a cloud of euphoria. True, the three bad men had escaped our clutch once again; but with the central fortress of Oman securely in our hands, what could they do? That monstrous tumour had been the cause of all our pain and sickness for a dreadful year and a half. Now, by brilliant surgery, Smiley had excised it. The Ancients said that he who holds Nizwa holds Oman, and he who holds the Jebel Akhdhar holds Nizwa. And there they were, exultantly on top: Sultan's soldiery, Life Guards, S.A.S., T.O.S., tribesmen, donkeys and all. Our allies drank their fill of the cup of victory by triumphing all over the plateau top and showing the inhabitants who was the winner. The British troops did not endear themselves to the native mountaineers; but that was not their purpose.

Elsewhere, too, we and our friends worked off a few sub-conscious hates by rampaging into all the villages we had not been free to enter before, and ransacking them for concealed arms and Imams, enjoying the cowed looks of our once-formidable foes. Sheikhs were treated with less than respect; those who had sat on the fence had their beards pulled—in one or two cases, literally; those who had been openly on the Imam's side were impounded; those who had tried to help us were often ignored.

These were intoxicating days. They were tonic enough for the temporary visitors who had wrought the victory; they were far more heady for us who had been through it for so long and who, because of our contracts, had to stay on, as in 1957, while the conquering heroes departed. David Smiley, Mike Read, and the other officers who had been posted into our army remained, but the S.A.S. and auxiliaries began to drift away home after they had completed their chastisement of the Green Mountain and their purges of the rebel villages. Any resemblance to August 1957 was ignored. We had won; we had the mountain. Colin Maxwell went up to live in Sharaija as resident conciliator, with the difficult job of seducing the mountaineers from their allegiance to the fiendish old reprobate who was their tribal chief, and attaching them to the remote tyrant who was their titular Sultan. He achieved a remarkable success.

This time I joined Mike Read's Muscat Regiment, stuffing my protesting head into a flat scarlet bonnet with a crimson puff-ball on top. Jasper returned to his freebooters at Sohar. I was also obliged, in the name of all that was military, to mow the beard I had grown in the days when Jasper and I spent more of our time on the Jebel than off it. Jasper's beard, a growth like black hay, held out longer than mine but in the end that also had to fall. We were to be no longer a clutch of enthusiastic eccentrics. We were to be proper officers, in a real Army, and we were to look the part. To this end, my red balmoral was a paradoxical contribution.

Mike Read was one of the rare real gentlemen I met in the Army—British or Sultan's. It had always been a mystery to me, ever since I first put on uniform at the age of seventeen, why so many military commanders found it quite beyond their power to be efficient and worthy of promotion without being thoroughly unpleasant. Some of them went further—"why be unpleasant," their motto seemed to be, "when with a little effort you can be absolutely impossible". This is why it was such a joy to find a commander who was in every way a model of what a military commander should be, and who was also a man of gentle charm who inspired affection as well as respect. Such a man was Mike Read; another was Eric Johnson. I always found it far easier to respond to the leadership of such men, than to the other kind, who regrettably seem on the whole to gain higher rank. Perhaps this quirk explains to a great extent why I am no longer in any sort of army at all.

Mike Read's regiment was made responsible for the coast and the eastern approaches to the Jebel. He sent me to Awabi, with an entire company of brand new, red-raw recruits straight from the Depot—Baluchis to a man, with their private language, which despite my mouse-gnawed book I had failed to master. He gave me two well-bred British captains to help me, both eager and willing to learn, and I had a fat sergeant-major of indeterminate sex who was also Baluchi but who, luckily, knew something of one of the recognized tongues of men—Arabic. We had no operational task. There seemed to be no longer any need for those, and now was a time for training, for schooling the boat-loads of recruits from Gwadur, for building the Sultan's army into what it had never had a chance to be before—a well drilled security force.

Awabi was one of the historical strategic strongholds of Oman. On the seaward side of the Jebel Akhdhar there were only two significant entrances to the plateau along its entire length; and here the Jebel flanks did not rise stark and straight skywards out of the plain, but were fringed by a wide skirt of black lava hills which if they had not been overtopped by the Green Mountain would have been respectable mountains in their own right. These also were penetrated by only two or three paths. Awabi lay astride the plexus where two of the routes through the black hills met to join in the approach to the plateau.

This ravine was altogether a more majestic canyon than those on the inland side. It contained whole villages, and vehicles—as we had learnt the year before—could drive right up to the very roots of the central tableland. The ravine at the base turned a right angle to run along the foot of the plateau; here it was a necklace of villages, and two or three separate staircases climbed zigzagging up the wall. The whole gorge was some twenty miles long.

In its mouth stood the small square fort of Awabi, with a yellow cluster of mud-box houses nestling in a bed of green palm groves a couple of hundred yards downstream. This little castle

was the home of the Governor of Awabi, a pleasant rustic gentleman who bit his fingernails to the bone and had no clear idea
of what went on. The fort overlooked, and so controlled, the
water channel which kept Awabi village alive. This was a magnificent piece of prehistoric engineering. The conduit emerged
from a tunnel in the very rock of the mountain—God alone
knows how the builders found a spring by driving a shaft into
solid rock. The water then promptly disappeared down a vertical
hole, like a well. Across the other side of the ravine there was
another well, up which the same water bubbled, to continue its
way to the village. It was a perfect syphon. There was no other
feasible way to cross the gorge, because a tumbling torrent of
water roared down it whenever there was a rainstorm on the
mountain, which would wash away any imaginable aqueduct.

Similar systems supply Nizwa, Rostaq, Ibri, and all the major
centres of population and most of the inhabited countryside. The
pre-Arab occupants of Oman, who built the steps up the Jebel
Akhdhar and constructed these fantastic waterworks, have as
their monument the whole land of Oman to this day—without
them it would be an uninhabitable desert, for usable natural
water is rarely encountered, and there is no natural route to the
moist uplands of the Green Mountain.

We soldiers did not live in the fort, but in tents and palm-
thatch huts around it. The sloping flank of the mountain rose
directly beside my back door, and thereon we sported with our
troops, teaching them tactics, fieldcraft, and rock-climbing. There
was a level terrace on the other side of the chasm which had been
cleared of stones during the campaign to make a rough airstrip,
and this we used as a parade ground. As at Tarif in 1955, I had
a virgin field to plough, with a sparkling new company of recruits. But these were different. These were Baluchis, spanking-
fresh from Baluchistan.

I had by this time seen a great deal of our troops' behaviour
under enemy fire, and I had ample empty days to ponder it.
The conclusion I reached was that we had always paid insufficient attention to the gulf between the ideas of warfare which
our soldiers inherited from their ancestors, and the European way

of waging war which we tried to impose upon them. The problem was similar to the struggles we had had in the primitive Trucial Oman Levies, trying to train aboriginal bedouins and goatherds. There the difficulty was of discipline and drill. Here it concerned fighting.

To an Arab or Baluchi, there is only one way of conducting a battle. He takes his gun, settles behind a rock, and shoots at his enemy. When his enemy shoots back, he ducks; when his enemy stops, he pokes an eyebrow round his cover and fires again. This goes on until darkness falls, or one or the other runs out of ammunition. The thought of getting out from cover and actually going *towards* the man who is shooting at him quite simply never occurs. Once behind his stone he clings limpet-tight, even against aerial bombardment; but that is mainly because he knows he is safer there than anywhere else.

I had noticed this on the early mountain patrols. Some advanced sentinel would be flinging an occasional bullet at us from several hundred yards away, to warn us that he was there in case we had any more aggressive ideas. He was so far away that he could do us no conceivable harm, he was not even trying to aim properly, and anyway we were wasting time, so I stood up to go on. My men looked at me as if I was mad; and it needed much eloquence to show them it was all right. They were not cowards, they just did not do that sort of thing if somebody was shooting at them. In time, when they had been shot at often enough, they grew as nonchalant as any seasoned soldier—and as quick to duck if the bullets got really dangerous. But this inhibition lost us valuable time, for it had to be overcome with every new recruit.

This, I mused, was a great drawback to any army, particularly one which is required to be offensive and not merely a *corps de garde*. Talib's men had the same weakness, but they were on top, and their only adventurous sallies—until they too became inured—were by night.

Knowing that the object of all drill is to inculcate in the soldier an entirely automatic response to certain stimuli, and to eliminate altogether his own intelligent reactions (and it is intelligent to stay down when shot at), I introduced an experimental type of training for these grass-green recruits assembled at Awabi. It was not at all my own invention, but the emphasis I placed upon it was unorthodox. Perhaps it was a futile experiment; my Awabi company was never required to go into action, so I have no idea whether it would have worked or not.

It derived from the old-fashioned Battle Drill of the British Army. A sequence of military movements was banged into the men, over and over again with horrible monotony, until it was as reflex as a knee-jerk. But the stimulus for this mechanism, in my lessons, was a shot: fired as close as I, or the instructor, dared—which in our unprincipled army was close indeed. (I had first tried this drill at Izki, where one soldier received his stimulus right in the buttock. But he thought we had done it on purpose, as punishment for idleness, and he merely went through his drill more briskly; so I had no need to apologize for the poor aim of the instructor).

This game was meant to teach the new soldier what it sounded like to be shot at closely enough to be really imperilled. We fired other rounds well over his head, or safely to the flank, and to those he was not supposed to react, but to maintain his plodding progress until he received an order. On the skin-skimming round, however, he was to go through his motions as taught—unthinkingly. He was to leap to cover, wriggle into a firing posture, raise an eye, locate the hostile marksman, set his sights, shoot back; he was to perform a series of mechanical actions to ensure an aggressive approach and to bring him, if geographically possible, into a position where he outflanked or overlooked his enemy. If he achieved that, his enemy would go away; of that there was no doubt.

We began this course on the airstrip parade ground, and in the early lessons we used a whistle or some other innocuous stimulus until they were ready for the more realistic one. My two captains had learnt the curriculum from me, and they carried it out, blowing whistles and gesturing with their canes to induce a smart performance.

All they induced was a mutiny.

Here I was again, I thought, remembering my "revolting soldiery" at Tarif. But at Tarif I had soldiers with whom I could communicate—my Arabic even in those days had been adequate for saying what I thought of insubordinate troops, and for ascertaining what was on their minds. But my only links with the soul of these mutineers were the primitive vocabulary of grunts I had managed to absorb from the *Grammar of the Baloochee Language*, and the epicene sergeant-major whose Arabic was only marginally better than my Baluchi.

They had been as good as gold all morning. The rebellion began after the midday dismiss. I was sitting in my leaf hut sharing a pre-lunch gin with the two captains and scarcely conscious of the familiar ground-swell of meaningless sounds from the soldiers' lines, when suddenly the rhubarb-rhubarb grew into a rumbling growl of inarticulate discontent. Before many minutes it was a tempest of wrath, the captains were visibly curious if not alarmed; I knew now what was going on, so I sipped my gin and allowed time for the sergeant-major to plunge into the eye of the storm and see what it was all about.

Soon enough, in he came, fat and formal as ever; he saluted, and began to report, while the querulous babel maintained a menacing accompaniment in the background.

"Soldiers say no parade," he explained.

We raised our six eyebrows in appropriate disapproval.

"Soldiers," he became more explicit, "say no parade—never." The chorus of unintelligible complaint seemed to corroborate this.

It was time to ask why. "Why?" I asked.

The sergeant-major, dark red and sweating after his strenuous efforts to find out why, could now do little more than suggest that one of my officers had hit one of the men. A glance at both their faces was enough to convince me that there had been no barbarity on that side, but it was a tedious piece of work unravelling the tangled thread of the sergeant-major's narrative.

It was the gesturing with the canes, so it appeared after much interrogation; their use as a kind of conductor's baton to whip spirit into the lethargic recruits. True, once or twice one of the captains had been impelled to do more than just gesture in the air, and had made physical contact with his man. But this was absurd : even in the British Army, there can be few drill instructors who never so much as touch a man, with hand or stick, to emphasize an oath or to enjoin greater zeal—and with us it was a daily occurrence, either to adjust a part of the body which was out of alignment, or to indicate a man whose name might have been Gom Dad Wali Dad when one's sense of the absurd inhibited its use.

But there was more to come. The sergeant-major was by now blushing like an overstoked stove. The incident complained of, he murmured in embarrassment, had concerned a part of the anatomy which. . . .

A horrible thought came at once into my mind, and as soon fled it, abjectly. My young men were of a robust kind more likely to respond to a female goat than a male Baluchi.

The sergeant-major saw me momentarily blench and hastened to reassure me. More by suggestive gestures than direct exposition, he indicated that the drill-instructor had poked one of the soldiers in the bottom with his stick, in order to help him on his way to a prone posture.

With the uproar showing no signs of exhaustion in the men's lines, I sternly avoided catching the eye of either of my officers, for fear of dissolution into helpless mirth. For it was so obvious that such a thing had taken place, not once but probably a hundred times—and my man shot in the arse at Izki had raised no mutiny. I told the sergeant-major to fetch me a spokesman with whom I could endeavour to converse on the subject. He waddled out.

Then followed a hiatus while he hurried back and forth, negotiating; first they said they would speak to nobody; then they said they would all come, all or none; then they demanded written safe custody for their champion; and so it went on. At length I sat at my office table looking at the defiant eyes of the speaker for the mutineers. I invited him to talk, in whatever language he chose.

To my relief he spoke Arabic of a sort, like the sergeant-major, who was now standing apprehensive at my shoulder. And out of his mouth gushed a torrent of complaints : grouses such as every soldier under heaven nurses tenderly in his breast, but loves too much to attempt their redress . . . however, these clodhopping Baluch were too simple to understand the mystiques of soldiering.

The food, the beds, the hours of work; sergeant-major, hot weather, hard drills; they had no pull-through cords, yet were required to clean their rifles (I made a note of that one); the sergeant-major, the hours of work, the food. It was like a psychiatric catharsis, or a purge of the bowels—I could see the man getting happier with every plaintive phrase. But still the distant thunder grumbled—and the spokesman suddenly remembered his duty to his fellows. They would go on no parade, he told me, almost sadly, until I dismissed the offending officer.

This was the first time he had mentioned this at all, and I pressed him to be more explicit.

But I failed. I never found out why they objected to him. The poke in the backside with a stick was a pretext, obviously, although in strict equity it was a valid one. As officers are judicially protected from assault by their men, so are soldiers judicially immune from even technical assault by their superiors. But this was footling. But it was all I got.

I replied slowly and at length, in order to ensure that the man understood and could relay what I said. My officer would stay, until I chose to dismiss him—which would not be at the request of the soldiery. The men would return to work, in good order, or they would be abandoned—they would get no food from any cookhouse I controlled, and if they seized control of their own cook and cookhouse, they would get no food after they had eaten up the stores—which were, luckily, due for replenishment. They would be marooned there, at Awabi, strangers in a hostile land—the hand of every loyal inhabitant of the Sultan's domains would be against them (this was a perversion of the true state of affairs, but I warmed to my harangue)—I and my officers would carry on with those who did choose to work, and if anyone raised a hand against us he would be hunted down—etcetera—the shaken man was sent back, in the company of the sergeant-major, to put across my point of view.

It was ridiculous, like the Tarif mutiny, but potentially explosive, and the four of us—assuming the sergeant-major stayed sane—were very small and few and lonely in the depths of Oman. If there had been any genuine grievance my argument would have stood no chance—but slowly we heard the hubbub die down, there was an occasional arpeggio of question and answer, a chord or two of disagreement, a drum-roll of assent. The poor fellows had no grievance; they just did not know the form. Faced with my imaginary retribution they gave in.

I then set about the text-book post-mutiny procedure. Always, say the wise ones, give in to the men on anything unimportant, or anything which you agree has been overlooked. Never acquiesce to the particular demand which was the pretext of the mutiny, on principle. Select a small but sufficient number of the more intelligent of the penitents, and subject them to punishment. Forgive the rest, if possible with tears running down your cheeks.

I issued pull-through cords, had broken beds repaired, told the cook to improve; the officer stayed on; the ringleaders were fined; and we all got back to work the best of friends. The Baluch were learning how to be soldiers, and their education took in all aspects of the military art, including how to grouse.

12

THE DREADED SHORTY

T AKING off his hat-like turban, Grock scratched his bald dome, fanned himself with much puffing, kicked a cushion into place with a horny toe and sat down and yammered at me.

The eloquent fingers interpreted what he was trying to say. What a long time since we had met, yes he remembered those sultry days at Mahadha, no there was no news. The return of the Sultan's army to Buraimi—or at least my part of it—was more than welcome.

For too long the old fellow had been a sort of weed in the garden, flying his Sultan's flag like a prince of San Marino, surrounded by all the arrogant appurtenances of the real power which Zaid wielded in the oasis, backed as he was by a prestige company of Trucial Oman Scouts. Poor old Grock had nobody but his mad household servants and his most unprestigious guards. He sat alone in Turki's old palace, ruling an almost deserted province, whence all the men of influence and position had fled with Turki, and which had been allowed to crumble into forlorn decay as a result of the Sultan's punitive neglect of his mutinous villages. All round him, in a contrast as conspicuous as it was deliberate, shone the rich and flourishing towns and farm-lands of the Abu Dhabi territory in the oasis; the people strode like lordly ones in white gowns and silk headdresses; there was a multitude of private vehicles; Zaid's Buraimi was on the edge of a boom—these were the days of the Abu Dhabi oil strike. But in the Sultan's part the only vehicles were spread in hopeless bits on the ground outside baffled mechanics' shops, the date gardens were blackened cemeteries of dead trunks, and the most lordly person was Grock.

It was a measure of the dreamy optimism of those post-war days that as soon as my company was reasonably house-trained it had been sent north from Awabi to show the Sultan's badge in Buraimi, where for so long no soldiers had been seen but the T.O.S. While we were about it, we also took over the garrison of Ibri, where for two years the Scouts had been care-taking to allow us to concentrate our meagre forces around the mountain. But now we were back; and it was a triumphant moment. The whole seaward side of the Jebel Akhdhar was stripped of troops: for why did we need troops there now? A few of Jasper's smugglers, by now assuming the form and accoutrements of a gendarmerie, were enough to see fair play there. The only reason the Northern Frontier Regiment kept its company at Izki was because they felt it a pity to abandon the beautiful wall. The important thing for us was to get back on our own Northern Frontier—it was a mere detail that it was the Muscat Regiment who went there.

Grock had been yelling for some time for a servant to bring refreshments, without any response. Muttering anathemas into his beard he shuffled out, and returned after a few moments with a tin of pineapple and a tin-opener which he was trying ineffectually to operate. Sitting down and puffing, he handed it to me to cope with. Then we dug companionably into the fruit. Grock's household was of the most hairy kind, and his housecarls were a bunch of buffoons. But Grock was his old delightful self.

My mission was to arrange for a contractor to supply us with meat and firewood and other necessaries, and for a builder to turn the house and out-buildings we had been allotted, into a barracks.

"I know just the man," said Grock. "My bailiff is the man to talk to on this." He shouted imperiously, and from another room a small man like a crab came scuttling in sideways, with a face the colour of mud and bulging wicked eyes.

"My bailiff," Grock introduced the crustacean affectionately. "Al Qasayer."

Shorty. There was a split second when I wondered—but of course the name was as common a tag for small Arabs as its equivalent in England. I shook his hand with scarcely a tremor, and we got down to business.

Shorty was invaluable, and we became great friends. He knew everybody, he could get anything done. I don't know how we would have managed without him. . . .

I had installed half my company, under one of the captains, down at Ibri a hundred miles to the south, where they were to get on with repairing the ravages wrought by the Trucial Oman Scouts and to make themselves familiar with the area. It is a known fact that never since the siege of Troy has any unit ever taken over from another without finding itself heirs to a disgusting mess, any more than any unit ever hands over a camp except in far cleaner state than they found it. It is a military tradition. So we had to clean up after the T.O.S.

Meanwhile I set up my headquarters in Buraimi with the plump sergeant-major and the other captain, and I was mainly occupied for some weeks with converting the mud-brick house and yard into military shape. We were anxious to develop our own private water supply, and poking about we discovered a disused well inside the main building. Shorty briskly unearthed a troglodyte with long arms who specialized in digging out old wells.

This gentleman stripped near-naked and vanished into the hole. I asked him his name. "Bdew," he said. I blinked. "Bdew?" "Bdew. Bin Sfoof." He went on with his shovelling, while I marvelled at his name. I came across some spectacular names in my travels—later I was to meet proud men who bore handles like Hezhaz, Haidh Hoodh, Dub, and even Tomato; but Bdew bin Sfoof remains my favourite. He spent day after day down this apparently bottomless shaft, shovelling up and ladling out the most astonishing quantity and variety of rubbish—it had obviously been used as a garbage dump by our predecessors, who were, I reminded myself smugly, none other than the Trucial Oman Scouts. Lorry after lorry travelled to the desert to dispose of this detritus, and slowly the muck began first to squelch, then to ooze, finally to drip. Bdew had struck water.

Bdew descended his rope for the last load. He was by now working chest-deep in liquid, and had to duck his head under for every handful of rubbish. "One more piece," his voice echoed hollowly up to us. There was a splash and a gurgle, then a tug on the rope, and we heaved. We looked. Tied on the end of the rope was a rusty, slimy, but clearly recognizable Elsan bucket. We thanked Bdew, paid him generously, and went back to drawing our water from the town conduit.

Apart from my leave, and my sojourn in Sohar, this was the first time I had lived in any sort of house for nearly two years. It now seemed more natural to perform my daily meditations in the fragrant out-doors and under the clear skies than to lock myself into a stuffy closet. Also there is much, physiologically, to be said for the knees-to-chest position. I achieved such suppleness that I could sit on my heels for half an hour, if necessary, waiting in comfort for inspiration. One feature of Buraimi which made it the most hygienic of Arab towns, despite the daily fertilization of its sand dunes, was a population of enthusiastic beetles. These animals were so keen that they were almost importunate; no sooner had one shown one's intentions by adopting the conventional position than they would come winging in in vibrant droves, and hover expectantly. And they were so zealous that by the time one had finished there was scarcely a vestige left behind. All that could be seen were squadrons of beetles toiling laboriously backwards, bowling their treasures away over the rolling desert. I never found out what they did with it.

My second year was settling to its close, and I prepared to go home on leave again.

Throughout this Arcadian idyll since the fall of the Green Mountain there had been nothing to ruffle the even surface of our lives. One or two mines had gone off on the Nizwa-Izki side, but they, without any ghost of a doubt, had surely been leftovers—mines buried too deep, perhaps, or perhaps a piece of gravel had worked between the plate and the detonator, postponing its explosion for months . . . nobody could be laying mines now, we had won, we were on top of the Jebel, it was all over. Suleiman, Talib, and the Imam had made their way to Dammam, we knew that by now—but they were defeated men. There had been odd reports, from Maxwell in his elevated governorship at Sharaija, of young men leaving home and vanishing, none knew whither; sometimes a whispered name—"Al Qasayer"—floated disembodied on the breeze; but there was nothing more, except these few obviously old mines, which were just bad luck.

It was while I was at Bait-al-Falaj awaiting my plane to fly home that the blow struck us square between the eyes, forcing us to open them wide and see what was going on.

My three tonner at Ibri had been blown up. On a stretch of road that was used frequently every day; on its first morning run. By a much larger mine than usual, because the driver had his thigh broken, and always you were safe in a three tonner—the poor fellow died on his way to hospital.

That mine was a new one, freshly laid, and laid outside the recognized battle zone. We walked about with a perpetual question mark on our faces. Had we, after all, won not the war, but only a battle?

I had my leave, and returned to an Oman and an army with all the triumph blown out of it and—so far—nothing but puzzled disappointment to take its place. We had, with extreme difficulty, climbed victoriously out of a conventional war with a shooting enemy and a recognizable front line, only to find ourselves up to the chin in a guerilla war with an invisible enemy, and a front line which was assuming two dimensions instead of only one—it was us against the whole country, not just the Jebel.

Or so we thought.

The idyll with Grock was over. My two months leave had seen my company extracted from its lotus-eating life at Ibri and Buraimi and pulled in to Bait-al-Falaj, which my Baluchis (whose language has no F or J) called Beetle Plug. The half-completed barracks at Buraimi were abandoned to the sand and the scorpions which had been its occupants before we came, and the cantonment at Ibri was handed over once again—as much to our unspeakable disgust as theirs—to the Trucial Oman Scouts, who found it, naturally, in a condition of filth.

Beetle Plug had become unrecognizably civilized since I had last lodged there. I had, for the first time in two years, a room with a floor and ceiling, electric light and running water, and access to a genuine pull-and-let-go. We dined, rather than fed, in a properly-appointed Mess, with white-coated Goan stewards and a Mess President, and menus on the table. I found there a rather desperate social life, which was also a break with the Bait-al-Falaj I knew—where the only social amenities had been somebody else's whisky bottle and talk about the Olympian Waterfield. I played bridge—with Bob Warner, a real old soldier with all the tricks of his kind, and Tariq, who played with an urbane polish and gave our card table an outlandishly regal air with his full robes, silver dagger, and general Caliph-like grandeur. We attended twee musical evenings with the bank manager in Muscat town, who tweedled to us on a sort of portable parlour organ; and we stuffed down gargantuan meals with the more than gargantuan representative of the oil company. We even made up play-reading parties and put on performances to bewildered audiences of Indians and Arabs who must have marvelled at English drawing-room comedy of a generation past. And we drank, and played gramophones—here Bob Warner shone like a star, he had a rare collection of the curious, the earthy, and the privately-distributed. And we drank.

Here at the hub were now gathered most of the old sweats. Jasper was there, having lost his gendarmes and received in compensation the demanding task of founding a navy—which he tackled with all the willingness of an Alfred the Great, and which was, at any rate, a change from being a flying group captain, a donkey-walloping major, and a commander of irregular preventive men. Bob Warner was in charge of almost all the administration of the forces, as official paymaster and unofficial comptroller and auditor-general—he was probably the only man apart from the Sultan of whom Waterfield was in some awe. The whiskery Pat Gray had gone to join another egregious army in an even more remote part of Arabia, and John Clarke—of the tragic countenance and liturgical voice—had taken his place at the depot. Richard Anderson rolled globularly around as second-in-command of the Muscat Regiment; he had seized control of the Mess, where he fed us like maharajahs, and he periodically shattered the newly-joined officers until they got used to his fulminating nature. Malcolm Dennison was back in intelligence wrestling heroically with the huge task of building up an intelligence service from rock bottom. Haugh of Haughcol had left us; otherwise we originals lingered on in our various peculiar hats.

These days were marked by a continuous succession of doctors, who arrived one after the other, smart and keen with their shiny black bags, and left us after a short while, on stretchers. The class of human being with the highest casualty rate of all was the medical officers. They used to take elaborate care of their own mortal clay, as an example to the rest of us whom they endeavoured to convert to their own precepts of hygiene. They tested every source of water which they feared might at some time reach their lips, subjecting it to elaborate chemical analysis and pronouncing it foul; the water then must be purged of its vileness by a drastic dose of chemistry before it could be admitted into the company of decent men. They waged war without quarter on flies and other forms of animal life, and they had all their fruit and vegetables ritually purified in permanganate of potash or some similar disinfectant. They were fanatically hygienic; and they succumbed like autumn leaves to every imaginable ailment of the alimentary tract. Those of us who, like Jasper, John Clarke, and myself, had been obliged by force of circumstances to drink goat-contaminated water alive with mosquito larvae, to eat whole meals of which the flies were a significant portion of the ingested nourishment, to share impure messes of dates with unwashed soldiers and diseased Arabs, the doctors' obsession with sanitary matters and their coincidental casualty rate was a source of much cynical amusement. In all the years I spent in Arabia, often under conditions of the most revolting uncleanliness, I never paid the slightest attention to the matter at all; and never for one single day was I off work sick. Perhaps I was just lucky.

Not only our hygiene was being ruthlessly improved. A special emissary from the War Office, a clever brigadier, spent many weeks in Bait-al-Falaj formulating recommendations to ensure that never again, even though the heavens fell, would British soldiers have to fight in Oman. We were given every opportunity to say what we thought we wanted, and to be told what the brigadier knew we needed: hence Jasper's navy, and hence also a new full-strength General Staff with people like brigade majors and D.A.A. and Q.M.G.s, signals officers and staff captains, who were now doing what in the old days Waterfield had done more or less single-handed. We even got our own air force, light propeller-pulled aeroplanes which could carry machine guns and bombs and which were flown by wildly enthusiastic pilots on loan from the Royal Air Force who knew they could never have such fun anywhere else on earth. Lots of new British Army officers came to us, and we also got some more mercenaries on contract, who were a counterweight—the old curds-and-whey split between the Sultan's officers and those of the Queen was still sadly apparent. The depot, meanwhile, filled with Baluch recruits; Jasper's old gendarmerie was transmuted into a police force under some ex-colonial policemen; we planted barracks over the length and breadth of Oman; and Waterfield benignly eyed his military empire grow luxuriantly beneath his feet.

Brigadiers and gilded staff notwithstanding, the period we were now entering was the worst of the whole campaign. We had won the war; but the raging plague of mines turned the victory to soot in our mouths. They were as bad as they had been in the darkest days of the rebellion, when Talib had made his bid to drive us off the roads. Talib was making another bid—but he was no longer in Oman; no longer could we hope and plan for a decisive military triumph to bring us peace of mind. We had had the triumph, but it had done us little good. Our gloom was partly pique at finding Talib and company militarily dead but resolutely refusing to lie down; it was more due to our nerve-grinding frustration at being able to do nothing whatever about it. At least, during our year and a half of Green Mountain, we had been able to work off repressions by patrolling, shooting big guns, calling up bombers: but now we had nothing, nobody to shoot at, nowhere to bomb. We were sitting ducks. The most sensible suggestion to emerge from this period was that we should simply stop driving around altogether: it seemed, to our jaundiced eyes, that all we were doing—despite our inflated General Staff, despite our air force, our navy and our gendarmerie—was to charge about the countryside of Arabia getting ourselves blown up, a thing which would never have happened at all if we had not been there in the first place.

The phantom saboteurs were using bigger mines regularly, now, of which the opening salvo at Ibri was merely a foretaste. They had given up trying to discomfit us with their usual toys, and were bringing really heavy anti-tank mines to bear: potent enough to disable a large tank, they made scrap metal of a Land-Rover, even our armoured ones, and blew the cab right off a three-ton lorry.

And throughout this time we gleaned not the smallest grain of a notion as to what was really happening. We read numberless reports from diplomatic bags that the dreadful three in Saudi Arabia were recruiting an Army of Liberation, but we could never find out anything palpable about it. As for the bangs and thumps which punctuated almost every day in Oman itself, the only reasonable assumption was that they were the work of local ill-disposed characters, using—we hoped—left-over stock from the war days. Proceeding on this assumption, we followed up every whisper, every rumour and myth; and the quest for Al Qasayer developed into an obsessional man-hunt. Whole towns were cordoned off and searched, houses ransacked, date-groves probed, for presumed caches of fireworks. Lists of devious persons were compiled, and anybody remotely connected by family or reputation with any of the known rebel leaders was regarded with the utmost suspicion. The Sultan promulgated a list of rewards which were to be paid to anybody—civil or military—who caught a gun-runner or a layer of mines or who discovered arms or explosives. These were tempting: a small mine could fetch its finder something like £125, which in a land where a labourer earned five shillings a day was a sum to dream about. He also decreed Draconian penalties for any village anywhere near where anything was blown up. And the army disposed its entire resources and all its time to patrolling the roads, trying with no success whatever to catch a mine-layer at his work.

All we asked was just one mine-layer. If we could catch just one, we felt, in our present mood, we would have justified all our efforts, and we would be able—by the application of well-judged pressure—to snap the mainstring of the whole subversive web which surely underlay the soil of all Oman.

And Al Qasayer . . . we heard so much about Shorty in these days that we were honestly convinced he was a one-man Maquis. Men said he was seen at times in Buraimi; he drove around, it was murmured, like a ghostly traveller, in a Land-Rover which appeared a different colour with every new report—a Flying Dutchman with four-wheel drive, laying mines. We sent up earnest prayers that one day, in Providence's good time, Al Qasayer would fall into our desperately clutching hands—Land-Rover and all.

Meanwhile, Grock's short-statured bailiff carried on his useful Government work, collecting taxes, controlling irrigation, traversing his bailiwick in one or another of the Sultan's un-uniform vehicles.

13

INVISIBLE MEN

IN desperation we tossed the military manuals—and all pretence of being an ordinary army—out of the window. Our leaders went into a huddle, and a new and *ad hoc* strategy was conceived. The plan which finally emerged from the womb of Bait-al-Falaj was twins. In the first place we thirsted for knowledge of what was really going on in the blank-faced towns and villages. Secondly, we itched to arrest a rebel *in flagrante delicto*. Normal military procedures were useless for either of these tasks: patrols grinding around the country in dust-generating convoys, or clattering and clumping through sleepy hamlets in ammunition boots, are not the most subtle of weapons. We had to be distinctly unmilitary in our approach. The blimps and the buffers protested with much twirling of moustaches, but the original minds had their way. Once more our good friends the Trucial Oman Scouts came bouncing down to relieve us of the more ordinary military duties, and the unleashed companies of the Sultan's army transformed themselves into a sort of wholesale Boy Scout patrol.

The process of getting our ears to the ground, the first part of the plan, left the more conventional company commanders speechless with grief, for they were summarily bereft of their most intelligent native officers and N.C.O.s. These were installed in "listening posts": small picquets, consisting entirely of high-ranking Arabs, set up in the major towns ostensibly as wireless stations for the Sultan's governors. Thus Rostaq and Awabi had one post apiece, who erected their aerials in the governors' forts and tapped away noisily at regular hours throughout the day. But the personnel were carefully selected. No moon-faced Baluchi, be he never so nimble-fingered on the morse key, was allowed within miles of them. Lieutenant Ali Mohammed, my first Jebel Akhdhar companion, was in charge at Awabi, and at Rostaq was installed a fat and avuncular Arab sergeant named Saif who had an acute mind and numerous useful friends in high and low places. Assistant operators and battery-boys were similarly choice men. They were encouraged to wear civilian clothes: to amble around the bazaar on their off-duty hours, which were many; to look up old friends, and to cultivate new ones. In a word, they were spies. The plan was childishly crude; but for so long the army had been little more than a cacophonous cavalcade of trucks and Land-Rovers rampaging over the countryside, getting itself blown up and storming through the nearest centre of habitation and tearing it apart, that this simple experiment of putting the sharper of our eyes and ears into focus paid off generously. It was only a few weeks before Sergeant Saif introduced me, on one of my routine visits to his radio station, to Zahar, an old friend he had known some years back and had met again at Rostaq: a man whose knowledge of rebel affairs, whose family connections with the highest rebel councils, and whose deep-rooted hatred of the Imam and all his tribe, were without parallel . . . in time this casual acquaintance developed into one of our main sources of intelligence.

Ali Mohammed at Awabi, too, found an old chum whom he had not seen for many moons, pacifically hiring out his donkey for the carriage of lucerne and indigo and whatever freight he could engage. This was a man who knew the little town and its environs inside out. Slowly, reluctantly, but—with increasing fluency, the insignificant donkey man released a flood of information: names of Talib's relatives, henchmen, supporters, and slaves; names of men who had joined Talib's banner in Dammam, and where they lived; descriptions of men we were trying to find, and of a hundred more we had never heard of.

Gently but surely we began to gather an idea of what we were being blown up by. Real names, real people, who actually lived and really went about the countryside planting bags and tins of

147

explosive, took the place of the faceless phantoms, the supernatural Al Qasayer, the anonymous "local dissidents" who were presumed to teem in every village in Oman. The reality emerged from the mists of ignorance. There were but a handful of active saboteurs; they lived, not in Oman, but with the exiles in Saudi Arabia; and they came and went at regular intervals. They travelled into Oman by a variety of quite innocent means, and planted their deadly seeds, and left again for a rest before their next assignment. We learnt the routes they used; the agents who helped them; the means they used to smuggle their loads through—or past—the customs; their places of sojourn in Oman. At last, we knew where we were.

And it was not long before the great day of days when we caught somebody. This was the fruition of the second branch of our strategy, which was grimly known as the Killer Squads.

My company, having lost its leading intelligentsia to the listening posts in Rostaq and Awabi, was made over to this interesting exercise, and I was given *carte blanche* to train them for it.

My ambition was to dispose groups of men out in the countryside, covering selected vulnerable stretches of road, in such a way that nobody except ourselves would know that there was anyone in the vicinity at all. The soldiers must scan the area thoroughly, by day and by night, and be able to creep up and snatch anybody they saw apparently messing about on the track. But no one would know they were there. In this way, we hoped, the mine layers would be soothed into a sense of security and one of them would attempt to plant his load with less care than if he thought there were military men around. And the moral effect of his being caught in the act would be electric, on his comrades and ourselves.

The problems were huge. The training must be consummate, the administration infallible. My men had to learn to conceal themselves perfectly, to move freely but unseen, to escape the notice of wandering goatherds passing near their lair, to cook and eat and live invisibly. They had to be disembodied eyes by day and ghostly patrols at night—and drastically effective if they saw or heard a target. They were, moreover, merely men : they had to be moved into position, supplied, relieved by fresh patrols, and no one must know they were there. . . .

We spent day after day in all kinds of country, practising the art of what would be called woodcraft if there had been any woods. In a nude and barren land like the hills of Oman, where the only trees are scattered leafless shrubs, the task was far more challenging than it may at first seem. We practised moving across a bare plain, where nothing but an occasional rock broke the dull brown landscape. The art here was not to hide behind anything, but to endeavour, with one's khaki clothing and brown skin, so to resemble from a reasonable distance the natural terrain as to be indistinguishable. The men did this under the eye of a watching instructor, keeping stone-still until they saw him momentarily shift his gaze, when they leapt or crept—as the chance allowed—for the next piece of shadow or stony ground.

I had them establish a hide in stark naked hills, and outwit the search party I sent to seek them out : the secret here was to keep a wary eye on the approaching hunters, and lie doggo; unless the searchers were unmistakably coming straight for them, when they must edge away, craftily, exploiting every smallest boulder or bush, keeping ever out of sight.

I led them to a stretch of road with low hills on either side; there they were to vanish, and I would set about scrabbling a hole in the road. My men had then to approach close enough to me to make my arrest certain, without my seeing them or hearing them. In bare desert this was high-grade fieldcraft. Then we tried night work. Moving in pairs, they patrolled the road, invisible and unheard but alert for any sound. One of the pair had a torch, the other his rifle. When they had worked close enough to their quarry the torch-man flashed his light and the rifleman aimed—and would, if needed, shoot.

The exercises were so realistic that towards the end the pseudo-mine-layer—myself or an N.C.O.—was almost invariably caught, genuinely unawares, both by day and by night.

The maintenance of these counter-terrorists caused a great deal of head-scratching. Frequent reliefs were impossible. Nor could the squad stay out for weeks. We decided on five days as a compromise. They must have bedding, rations, water, ammunition, medical kit—there could be no sick parade for these soldiers— enough for five days, and they must exist without so much as a whisp of smoke or a whispered word. The ration was specially designed. It included tinned sardines, dates, and a peculiar chappatti which stayed moist and fresh indefinitely. The chappattis raised a problem of their own : there was only one place where this special delicacy was made, and only one woman we could approach to make it—she worked non-stop for about a week fashioning these unique pieces of bread. We produced some pretext or other. But they had to be prepared in large job-lots—if we returned to the good woman every five days for more, there would be gossip and speculation. We obtained smokeless fuel cookers from the Army, with which the men could make tea, and we composed a rudimentary medical kit including morphine syrettes in case someone started to yell. We bought suitably bucolic clothes so that at a pinch if seen from a distance they would look like yokels.

Finally, there was the riddle of how to place the squad in position—having selected a position where they had a reasonable chance of carrying out their assignment; and there was the question of how to effect their relief. We mulled over a cluster of ideas, considering and rejecting camels and even goats as load-carriers.

Finally we struck a plan which involved no such extraordinary resources.

My whole company lurched bodily and noisily into the area between Rostaq and Awabi, which had been selected for this operation. There were about twelve miles of particularly wicked mine-country here, and two squads were allotted to watch it. The company gallumphed over the area in a sort of exercise-cum-patrol, such as the inhabitants were used to—dust boiling in clouds, clumping soldiers' feet shattering the midday quiet. Then we withdrew, satisfied, to a base about twenty miles away towards the coast, where there was water and a small hamlet. Known only to ourselves, the company when it withdrew was not at its full strength. Two killer squads had been left behind in the hills.

At the base the company settled down to an interminable, unnecessary, but plausible, chore—clearing and marking an airstrip.

It was then announced—*de par le Sultan*—that the Awabi-Rostaq area was a danger-zone, in which peaceful citizens had nothing to fear provided they went on their way directly and openly, but that anybody moving at night, or indeed anybody appearing to tamper with the road even by day—and a man squatting at the roadside for purposes of nature could look highly suspicious from a distance—was liable to be shot, with any needful questions being asked afterwards. This sort of announcement had been made before, and nobody was particularly bothered.

So we passed the days constructing our airstrip, and nobody went near the Awabi-Rostaq road at all . . . except that every five days a lorry drove after sunset to the outskirts of Rostaq where, apparently, it collected firewood or some other necessaries for the camp. In fact, it waited until two dark files of men came looming silently out of the night, and the original fire-wood collectors had disappeared into the gloom of the Awabi road to take their place. The lorry returned with a different set of faces, which none but a preternaturally observant Arab could have noticed, and the change-over was complete for another five days.

The results of this experiment were interesting, if no resounding success. The post nearer to Awabi was exposed fairly soon after its installation, due to the stupidity of a member and the patriotic fervour of the people of Awabi. A soldier was taken sick and he elected to make for the listening post at Awabi for succour. On his way, dressed as he was as an Arab, his devious and shifty progress aroused suspicion in a native who happened to see him emerge from the hills. This worthy summoned what was virtually a posse to scour the area. There were, as far as anybody knew, no known soldiers in the neighbourhood : who, or for what, this skulking Arab might be, required investigation. So to the horror of the Killer Squad, coiled resting in the heat of the day in its niche in the lava hills, probably trying as best it could to brew a cup of tea without so much as the clank of a mess tin, out of Awabi came pouring a purposeful body of citizens, armed to the eyebrows, which proceeded to sweep over the hills like a flood tide. Not even the rigorous training they had undergone could avail my men against this mass onslaught. They were exposed, sheepish, and retired with as much dignity as they could find, to Awabi, explaining that they were on a training exercise and meant no harm.

The Rostaq squad was similarly sought, but their story was different. In this case it was the inquisitive noses of a handful of amateur sleuths in the town, which endangered their seclusion. One or two of these curious characters began to ask themselves : how does it come about that the Government warns of death to anybody who so much as squats to relieve nature, on the Rostaq-Awabi road, while at the same time it takes pains to show that there are no soldiers in the neighbourhood at all? How can they enforce this rigorous measure without guards or patrols? Where are the men to shoot us if we pause for a pee? Those uniformed coolies clearing the airstrip twenty miles away cannot do any-thing—if they are in fact doing only that . . . the process of de-ductive thought flowed freely in these fertile minds, and they came to the conclusion that probably things were not as they seemed. Perhaps there were soldiers, after all, grazing goat-like in those baking hills. Let us, they exhorted themselves, go and have a look.

So indeed they did. For the best part of two weeks, small groups of detectives went out from Rostaq to see for themselves if their deductions had been correct. Day after day they came, and prowled around the hills, and taxed every resource of the embarrassed Killer Squad : which contrived, by consummate fieldcraft, to remain undetected. The detectives finally abandoned their quest, baffled.

My killers never caught a mine layer; but nor, for the whole period of the exercise, was there a mine in the area; and when, after the operation had been called off, word was allowed to leak into the populace of what we had been doing under their noses, the frightening thought of spectral soldiers stalking darkly through the mountains had an inhibiting effect on the mine layers' activities for a long time afterwards.

14

A BLACK BOOK AND A BIG LOG

T H E smelly old man who told me stories of taxis and shepherds at Sohar to get his impounded rifle back, had been relegated to the dimmer limbos of my mind for almost a year. He was just one of my many futile disbursements of Intelligence Funds.

It was while I was reading a jubilant report from the company commander on the Ibri side of the mountain that the grizzly face popped up into my mind's eye.

For the Ibri company's patrol had done it. They had caught a mine layer; or very nearly. The impossible, the inconceivable dream had at last come true. We had really got somebody with a mine.

This was not quite a Killer Squad coup as we had planned it; in fact it was the company commander himself, one Nick Carter—a professional soldier, much as a prize-fighter is a professional boxer—who was out on a routine Land-Rover patrol when he spotted a small group of cameleers belting through the hills with no obvious reason for their haste. With a feeling that this was just one more of those dreary daily checks, he called on the caravan to heave to. Instead it piled on more sail and made for the horizon—whereupon Carter aimed a shot or two across its bows which hit some men and a camel and caused it to stop. In the ensuing confusion one man scampered for the rocks and was lost, but the rest of the catch was a prize such as we had never seen. There in the saddle bags of the camels were mines, carefully wrapped up in sacking so as to look like something else.

The capture in human terms comprised one old man and a boy. Carter bore his prisoners triumphantly back to Ibri and questioned them, where after a decent interval they produced a pathetic account of innocence seduced and misled. The missing man, said they, had hired them, who were poor cameleers scraping up a mean but honest livelihood plying for hire. Their companion had engaged them to transport him, with baggage—contents unknown, but, they presumed, domestic—from a shepherd's encampment near Sohar to a place on the northern part of the Jebel Akhdhar near Balad Sait. Could they go, please; they needed to get back home, for the sake of their widowed mothers and hungry children. They would of course be most careful next time to ensure they were not carrying anything of which His Highness the Sultan might not approve.

This was just such a tale as might have been almost believed, but my colleague in Ibri was humanly reluctant to let go of anybody—even the camels—which constituted visible proof of the greatest success of the whole miserable campaign. More questions were pressed: and in the course of the quizzing the name of the shepherd who lived in the camp near Sohar dropped casually on to the pages of the interrogation report, where I a little later—just as casually perusing the cyclostyled sheets—spotted it. It was Harib bin Saif bin Bashir al Bida'i. My aromatic informer at Sohar had told me he was intructed in Sharjah to transport explosives to Harib bin Saif bin Bashir al Bida'i of Sohar. With a name like that there could be no question of coincidence. Here at last, slowly uncoiling itself in my mind, was a tenuous thread of thought.

Quite by chance, it was at this point that Mike Read relieved me of my company—still lurking watchful among the black hills of Awabi—and appointed me Regimental Intelligence Officer of the Muscat Regiment. This had nothing to do with my recollection of Harib bin Saif, which I had barely mentioned. It was part of a major offensive all along the front to improve our intelligence deployment. Our masters—Smiley and Waterfield, and the British brass hats in Bahrein—had seen clearly that what we now needed, before anything else, was a well-run and strongly manned intelligence. With the full backing of the British Government, who saw in this the only hope of stifling future Talibs in the cradle, expansion went ahead. One or two like myself with fair knowledge of the land were appointed I.O.s, and others, who had no knowledge of Oman but had mellifluous Arabic accents and strange ways, were posted in as District Intelligence Officers. Their task was to anchor themselves at places like Nizwa and Ibri, cut themselves off from mundane affairs and all temptations of the flesh, and do nothing all day and all night but talk to Arabs and try to penetrate the leaden curtain which so solidly separated us from the people.

Knowing nothing at all about the art of intelligence or its mysteries, I decided to hew from the bottom up. Although my parish, as Muscat Regiment I.O., was only that part of the country covered by Mike Read's troops—the seaward side of the Jebel Akhdhar, including Sohar and Awabi—I burrowed through every piece of paper I could find in the dusty attics of Bait-al-Falaj fort, to compile a list of meaningful names. Piling heaps of files, reports, and dirty pieces of paper (our usual stationery in the very early days) on a six-foot table, and heaping volume after volume of preserved signals on the floor about my feet, I spent a week going through the lot, noting down every single Arab who had ever been committed to writing. I jotted against his name a short scribble about what had been said about him at the time. As the days went by I accumulated a mass of some two or three hundred names, which I then sorted into alphabetical order and inscribed in a big black book. Thus under "A" I preserved characters like Ali al Aufi, "said to be mine layer": followed in the margin by a codified key to every reference to that gentleman I had been able to unearth in my burrowings. Talib, the Imam, and Suleiman bin Himyar I ignored, and one or two other notables—there was no need to compile a dossier of evidence against them. What I was after was a serviceable reference book, a Who's Who, to all the otherwise unattached names I would expect to hear whispered and tattled about in the ensuing weeks. Harib bin Saif was there; I disinterred his indictment from a report I myself had sent in from Sohar, recounting my first faltering steps in counter-espionage, along with the other personae in that still-

155

born coup: the taxi driver, the agent on the Sharjah side, and all. Al Qasayer had almost a whole page to himself, and in the end I gave him up as so many of his deeds were obviously apocryphal or patently conflicting. But on the whole I worked to the principle of including rather than excluding, at this early stage in my career.

My next step was to go out into the country, bearing my black book under my arm, and meet people. To raise the curtain, I sought out Ali Mohammed and Sergeant Saif, those spurious wireless operators who were still faithfully telegraphing, gossiping and spying from the listening posts in Awabi and Rostaq. Pretending to inspect their wireless installations, or to be delivering their pay, I joined them companionably on their respective straw mats and asked them if they had heard mention of so-and-so or not. Receiving the expected shoulder-shrug, I charged them to keep their ears open, and if the opportunity arose to ask after my characters: where were they, where did they live when at home, who were their friends and associates, what did they look like.

This was baby stuff, but like most babies it grew up, slowly and not without a considerable amount of protest. I got to know, in quite an off-hand way, Saif's friend Zahar, the one with the useful connections and the even more useful hatreds; I gained the confidence of Ali's donkey-friend at Awabi. I held the same sort of conversation with these two, when the time was right; I asked the same sort of questions and gave the same instructions.

With every visit the exercise became easier. I used to travel the circuit once a week, taking in half a dozen other places where there was no listening post but where I made and cultivated the acquaintance of the local Government man. Once in a while, by spilling a carefully-chosen name into the conversation, a snippet of news or a morsel of rumour would come bouncing back. It was all grist to my mill. Nor was it all a one-way traffic. Most of the names in my black book—which I had compiled in the first place from the raw material of gossip and suspicion, sedulously accumulated—would be of no significance to my host: some were genuinely respectable citizens, some were unknown goat-men, some indeed were imaginary; in this way, however, the

Government officials learnt a little of the cast of the drama, and were able thereafter to prick up their own ears at the mention of a significant name.

I passed several months in this way, catching no mine-layers but learning a great deal about them. I paid occasional calls on the other side of the mountain, where I renewed old acquaintances from our Ibri and Buraimi holiday, and added to my store of knowledge. There was the rare moment of excitement when a casually dropped name struck a chord in my memory, with a twang, like Harib bin Saif : for example, the man who got away from Carter's ambush had been recorded on a long-forgotten report from Ibri as "allegedly setting up saboteur squad in Dammam". Neither of these facts meant much by themselves, but taken together they were more than doubled in significance, and particularly they gave a clue to the reliability of some of the innumerable willing tongues we had to hear. In the same way as the Harib story gave a hall-mark to my Sohar friend when Carter's prisoners named him too, so did this other bit of corroboration from Ibri enhance a hundredfold the value of the voice which had first mentioned the man, over a now forgotten cup of coffee a year and a half before. For a gossip whose tittle-tattle has been confirmed by another story is at once promoted from rumour-monger to potential "reliable source". I found the discovery and correlating of cross-pollinations like these a most exciting pursuit.

By this process, I not only refined my black book into a fairly pure—though tenuous—essence of sound fact, but sifted the amorphous heap of informers into those who knew nothing and told us all they knew, those who knew a lot but kept it to themselves, and those rare men—jewels beyond price—who knew it and told it. Without this double-checking we had absolutely no way at all of knowing who was which.

While I was amateurishly working up my shapeless mass of information into some sort of serviceable form, others were doing the same, far more professionally and with greater finesse. These were the expert District Intelligence Officers, who unlike me had the cure of no large parish but were confined to specific areas in which to exercise their talents. These clever young men enjoyed a completely free rein—they were not even a part of our army, they were a tentacle of the Government, who paid them and demanded nothing in return but a copy of their reports. This caused an occasional flurry of embarrassment when we discovered, by devious means, that some of their reports were not being copied *in toto* to us but were reaching us in bowdlerized versions leaving out what the author thought of the service he was working with . . . but on the whole the D.I.O.s played fair.

We heard many strange tales of the D.I.O.s. One of them dressed himself up quite literally in a cloak and dagger—a black Arab muslin cloak and the uniform belly-knife of Oman—and squatted scratching himself in the market place of Ibri. There he sat, day after day, flapping his ears discreetly at every passing group of gossipers, until one morning the Governor's Audience was enlivened by a party of petitioners who demanded to know why the Government allowed a Christian to sit in the market place doing nothing all day, dressed up as a Trucial Sheikh. Should the Sultan not be apprised of this impertinence?

Another of these specialists was engaged to meet a spy. He appointed the time—at dead of night; he appointed the place— the third palm tree from the left. He arrived well before the hour, to make sure all was hushed and dark—when with a horrified flash of insight he realized he was about two feet too tall for an Arab. No matter how richly he bedecked himself in shawl and robe, dagger and cloak, his elongated form would betray his infidel birth. There was no time to lose . . . calling for a spade he dug a hole in the sand, two feet deep, and by the time his contact arrived the D.I.O. was down to his knees and the top of his head was level with that of his interlocutor. After the meeting, there were no eyes to see as he heaved himself out of the ground like the resurrection of the dead.

When my old company abandoned its Killer Squad enterprise, it was glad to be allowed to stay on in the area, which it had got to know with almost indecent intimacy. Rostaq was an important nodal point, a launching pad for further experiments and a base for dominating the north-eastern flanks of the Jebel Akhdhar. It was, moreover, one of the loveliest places in all

Oman, cool with moist green palm groves and mossy water-channels, white and pink with oleanders and roses, sweet with lime-trees and evening jasmine. The officers found constant fascination in the bazaar, where they could buy brass coffee pots, swords in silver-chased scabbards, and red and black goat-hair rugs for a few coins; in the grand and crumbling old castle, on its pyramid of rock, rising like a volcanic island from the surrounding sea of green fronds, with here and there a high barred window from which—if one was lucky—a pair of dark and wistful eyes could be seen gazing from the harem-prison out to the forbidden world of men. For the soldiers it had even greater charms : there were innumerable bawdy houses, and uncountable accommodating women.

I liked Rostaq, and I visited it once a week on my rounds. But sure enough, one day there was an early morning crump and a bazaar lorry tossed away its front near wheel while grinding through the outer environs. My arrival followed this misfortune by a few minutes—otherwise, of course, I might have hit the mine myself. Here was my first big challenge : I was supposed to find out who dunnit. I rolled up my sleeves and got my sleuthing-irons out and went to work.

For a start, I asked Sergeant Saif to send somebody to locate his friend. I never really expected Zahar to come out with the name and address of the mine layer, and nor did he. But he had some ideas. Meanwhile the Governor had sent along a bent-backed old man with a questing nose, who purported to be a tracker; and this blood-hound had, during my wait for Zahar, been probing with his proboscis in and around the area of the explosion.

The result of all this research was a squad of troops bucketing out to a small shepherd's encampment a mile or so off the road, whither they had been directed by the tracker's demonstrative nose and where, also, a small fringe of Zahar's blanket of suspicion had whisked. In they came in triumph, bearing a tragic-looking greybeard who wailed continuously of his shepherdless flock and manless family. We hardened our hearts. The finger of evidence had clearly and unhesitatingly marked him out as the man who had given shelter to the so far anonymous mine

159

layer. Zahar had denounced him—among, it is true, about two dozen other likely collaborators; but the tracker's nose had followed irrefutable footprints right up to his brushwood home, and out again the other side and into the pathless hills.

I tried my hand for the first time at interrogation. I later attained a fair degree of familiarity with this abstruse art, of which interrogating Omani Arabs is one of the more recondite branches; but this was my initiation. I came up against a solid wall, composed of three interlocking courses.

The first was the Arab's inborn inability to disentangle truth from falsehood, fact from fiction. A European in similar circumstances might attempt to bluff, to lie, to dissimulate for a while but when his version of the facts has been manifestly shown to him to be untrue, and he has been convinced that his interrogators know that it is untrue, he retreats into silence : he tells his tormentors that he has nothing to say, his lips are sealed, they may do their worst but he will utter no word more. But not an Arab : not, at any rate, an Omani shepherd. He will continue to swear the most impassioned oaths that he has six fingers on each hand, that the sky is green, until the end of his days. So with my suspect. The evidence of the footprints, shouting as loud and as clear as a Muezzin that he had received a visitor during the night, was simply contradicted : he did not try to say that the visitor had been a debt collector or his long-lost uncle : he just said he had not had one. He was like another suspect I interrogated later, when I was getting case-hardened; this one had clear and unmistakable stamps of entry and exit through Bahrein in his passport; yes, it was certainly his passport; no, he had never let it out of his sight; but Bahrein? He had never set foot in the place in his life.

The second impenetrable block was the Faith. Here I met again what I had faced, and wrestled with and subdued, in the early days in Sharjah : an overwhelming temptation to scream when at every turn in the conversation the name of God was brought in as a hedge. It was useless to ask the old goat-man any too pertinent question. He would say, simply and incontrovertibly, "God knows". Pressed, by my suggestion that doubtless God knew but he knew too, he muttered, "God is the best knower".

Threatened with the most hideous of fates if he persisted with his denials, he curled himself up comfortably in the thought that All was in the Hands of God. Asked about the mine, he explained patiently that it, like everything else that occurred on this created earth, was the Will of God.

Finally there was his old age and his congenital fatalism, against which no appeal, no threat could avail. A younger man, I later learnt, could be persuaded to ponder hard the prospect of a life in prison, to weigh it against the indulgence his co-operation could buy; provided the bargain was put convincingly enough, it was often accepted. But with this crumbling grey man there was no way out through that door. His dessicated and goat-ridden life, with all the sap long since dried in his veins, was not worth the coin I offered.

I handed him over to the Governor.

The Governor maintained, in the entrails of his castle, a dungeon; and in that dungeon there lay in wait, like a tamed but hungry beast of prey, an engine called the Maqtara. Two days of the Maqtara was generally enough, the Governor genially informed me as he took charge of my prisoner; a week in extreme cases. He told me of a man who had without any vestige of a doubt murdered his wife. His guilt was beyond dispute. But some quirk of Omani law demanded in his case a deposition from himself, and in this the murderer refused to oblige. So he was handed over to the Maqtara. Many weeks later he was released, having (according to local opinion) if not admitted, at least purged his crime. He was a helpless cripple for the rest of his days.

To this persuasive machine the Governor committed my intractable goat-herd. He submitted with no more than a patient observation that it was the will of God. Sergeant Saif of the listening post, who was a gentle and kindly man, visited him every day, morning and evening, exhorting him to release, if not the whole truth, at least as much of it as we obviously knew already : the man had still not admitted that the footprints were those of any human, or even any natural, agency, or that there were any footprints at all. But it was to no avail. His resolve set harder, the harder his joints congealed.

L   161

I also paid him regular calls. His dungeon was completely dark, except for the brief moment when the door was opened. He sat composedly on a heap of straw, which was his couch, his bed, and his lavatory, as it had been for his countless predecessors. The Maqtara was merely a massive block of wood. It was about six feet long, and some three feet wide and thick: from what colossal tree it derived was not known, it was so old that its birth and provenance were lost, but presumably it dated from the days when the Sultans and Imams of Oman had access to all the forests of Africa and could take their pick. Through this huge beam two holes had been bored. Peering pathetically through the other side were the prisoner's two knobbly grey feet linked together by a heavy iron shackle. The width of the beam was such that he was quite unable to flex, much less to exercise, the muscles of his legs: the knees were locked stiff: all he could do was waggle his toes. After a while a rigor would set in, the joints would set hard as in the most extreme arthritis. Set beside him on the straw was his lunch: a tin dish of black and adhesive dates, and a tin jug of comparable coffee.

He was always scrupulously polite. We greeted each other with all the formality of a Sultan's levee. Gravely, we asked each other how we were; as courteously, we assured each other that we were, thanks to the grace of God, well. We exchanged news; or rather, after the immemorial Arab fashion, we conveyed to each other that there was no news. He had no complaints, he told me. His guards were unexceptionable. His lot was the will of an Other than they. He bore me, in particular, not the smallest particle of illwill. But nor did the tiniest shred of information pass his lips.

We kept him there for a few days, the Governor and I; long enough to convince ourselves that he was quite prepared to stay there until the end of his life, which was miserable enough in any case and was only more uncomfortable in the Maqtara by reason of the restriction of his legs. We let him go. Wishing us a graceful farewell, he hobbled out blinking into the sunshine, having suffered no lasting harm. We met him often after this, placidly watching his flock by the roadside, and he always greeted us as warmly respected friends.

It was now over six years since I had first come to Arabia; but

162

the Arab character became more of a mystery to me the more it revealed itself.

While I was still I.O. of the Muscat Regiment I had my first sight of the inside of Jalali. Jalali was the Sultan's prison in Muscat harbour. It was the most feared thing in the whole of Oman; the mention of its name could bring conversation to a dead stop, it had an aura which the Bastille must have worn in the France of Richelieu, or the prisons of Torquemada's Spain. To Jalali had been committed the murderers of Otto Thwaites in Buraimi in 1953. Those who had never seen the place cursed the ridiculous clemency of the Sultan. Nobody who has been inside Jalali had anything but awe for the sentence.

Jalali was built by the Portuguese when they occupied Muscat in the sixteenth century. It is a grey fortress on a crag of black rock in the harbour. Muscat harbour is a desolate inlet, ringed with naked jagged hills of congealed lava, studded here and there with a mouldering castle or watch-tower. As the heat of day builds up, the circle of mountains almost glows with radiant heat which reverberates in shimmering waves back into the steaming pool of the anchorage, with Jalali as the focus. There is sometimes a soggy breeze, warmly odorous with decaying fish. The fastness of Jalali is connected to the sea front at low tide by a stinking strip of beach, but as the tide comes in it becomes an island, rising forlornly from the oily grey sea.

The walls all round overlook stark cliffs and the only way in, or out, is by a vertiginous flight of steps which terminates in a block-house dangling precariously over the sea. Inside, on top of the rock, is an open space, flanked on one side by a row of massive cannon pointing out to sea through arches in a wall, and on the other side by a blank crumbling stone façade pierced here and there by a barred window. Its high blind face has the unutterably forsaken aspect of some tall grey Glasgow slums. But the worst thing of all is the silence.

The guards at Jalali were found by the Muscat Regiment, and an officer had to visit them. Apart from the Muscat Regiment duty officer, that battalion's C.O., the medical officer and the High Command, nobody was allowed to see the miserable place.

I had no wish to repeat my excursion; I felt physically depressed and mentally sick. The ordinary prisoners were permanently shackled with ponderous iron bars between their ankles. The tiny water ration, in that steaming furnace, must have been a tantalizing mockery. More important prisoners were kept in perpetual solitary confinement. The roll of these included a vague uncle of the Sultan, who had spent almost all his adult life in Jalali to subdue an addiction to drink; a remote cousin of the Sultan, whom I had known in the Trucial Oman Levies as a truck driver, and who had later caused offence by going around the country saying what he thought about his august relation; a son of Suleiman bin Himyar, captured at Nizwa in 1957, and the unfortunate but too-trusting Ibrahim bin Issa, who had requested an interview with His Highness after his aborted rebellion in the Sharqiya in 1956. There was a celebrated madman, who greeted all British visitors with a heart-felt "God Save the King" and the waving of an imaginary Union Jack. There were the murderers of Otto Thwaites. And there were innumerable convicted felons whose crimes ranged from lese-majesty to debt. The whole place seemed to wail silently in the hopeless leaden heat.

Jalali was a word to work miracles with, to brandish as the ultimate threat in the face of an unhelpful captive. So far I had had only the Maqtara at Rostaq and the vague menace of unspecified doom to help me in my investigations. But my next appointment gave me the keys, so to speak, of the awful Jalali itself; and with the power not only to threaten but to use this appalling weapon I felt better equipped to become the Sultan's chief intelligence officer.

15

TWO IMPROBABLE TERRORISTS

AL HABSI was a sorcerer from Tanganyika. His father had been an Omani Arab and his mother a black African, and his magical talents were inherited from both the dark continent and Araby. He had a face like a Guru and Svengali eyes. He was practising as a dilettante merchant and part-time diamond smuggler in Tanganyika while the Talib troubles were on, of which he had heard nothing when one day he picked up the trail—by what occult means nobody knows—of a man who owed him some money. The trail, which he pursued with a single-mindedness entirely preternatural, took him to Dar es Salaam, on to a dhow bound for the lands of incense, up to the coasts of Oman south of Muscat, ashore and through the many-coloured hills and feathery woods of the Sharqiya and to the very foot of the Jebel Akhdhar. His magnetic eye led him ineluctably on, into one of the mile-deep gorges and up to the foot of the embattled plateau.

This was where his daemon deserted him. He was set upon by Talib's picquet and whisked up the nearest stairway to Sharaija, where he was summarily clapped in irons and incarcerated in a cave.

There followed a prolonged imprisonment, during which his captors strove to convince Al Habsi that he was a spy for the Christians and that he should confess. Al Habsi resisted, saying that he had come to collect a debt; and after a while his daemon returned to his bosom. He had brought with him from Tanganyika, sewn up in the hem of his robe, a substantial sum of money which had eluded his captors and which he contrived to exchange for the release of his ankles and a guide down the mountain.

He emerged, like an embodied spirit, at Awabi, where he was again arrested, this time by the soldiers of the Sultan who tried hard to suggest to him that he was a spy for Talib and that he should confess. The buoyant Habsi floated once again to the surface, convinced his new custodians that he was in fact merely an errant diamond smuggler from Tanganyika—a tribute to his mesmeric powers—and he was delivered up to the kindly Colin Maxwell, who interrogated him extensively about what he had seen and heard while a guest of the unholy Three.

Thereafter he was taken on to the payroll as an irregular undercover agent, and in the course of time he attached himself to me when I was made Force Intelligence Officer.

My new job had been deliberately left uncircumscribed, and I was free to do exactly as I liked, where and when I fancied, provided only that I produced at reasonably frequent intervals some sort of useful information. My territory was the whole of Oman, and my task was to establish contacts with the underworld, to visit the various parochial intelligence officers and try to mesh their individual efforts into a coherent whole, to interrogate prisoners, and to produce weekly, monthly, and quarterly reviews of the security situation for dissemination to our units and submission to superior plexuses in British Army and Foreign Office systems.

Al Habsi became my sinister familiar, and for a while, until his name and face and the stark terror they inspired in the superstitious Omanis became too notorious and the edge of his potency was blunted, Al Habsi was worth a whole secret service by himself. I used him mostly on interrogations. A man thought or known to be one of Talib's operatives would be locked up in a cell and consigned to Al Habsi's company for as long as need be. By merely squatting on the floor of the cell and talking to the unsuspecting captive, my famulus painlessly extracted a number of hitherto oyster-like secrets, which he then passed on to me to incorporate in interrogation reports for which I was generously praised.

166

Two Improbable Terrorists

One day we met a peculiarly obstinate specimen. I knew without a ghost of a doubt that Issa had been one of Talib's soldiers during the Jebel Akhdhar battles; I knew with equal certainty that he had since been trained by the exiles in divers military arts, and had been recently sent home to his village to await Der Tag. I had a complete dossier on the man, and, thanks mainly to one of the District Intelligence Officers' investigations, I knew as much about Issa as I did of Waterfield. But never a word he said. It was Rostaq and the shepherd all over again. He did not clam up and have "nothing to say"; he answered all my questions with the greatest courtesy, but with even greater mendacity. When pressed too hard he burst into tears and brought the interview to a heart-rending close.

Even Al Habsi could do nothing with him, by ordinarily hypnotic methods.

So Al Habsi dug down into the obscurer corners of the Omani pharmacopoeia and came up with a Truth Drug. This was a brown powder, compounded of some vegetable from his own district; which deserves medical analysis. Its power was staggering— and Al Habsi was not its complete master.

I had the stuff stirred into Issa's tea, Al Habsi assuring me it was tasteless, and sure enough the prisoner drank his tea without a blink. Then Al Habsi and I waited in my office, counting out half an hour by our watches, allowing time for the drug to work.

When the time had come we crept down the stairs and out to Issa's cell. Al Habsi tip-toed in, I followed. I stood unobtrusively in the corner while Al Habsi got down to work. Gently, with a voice like a muted Mesmer, he led the prisoner back in time, as a psychiatrist takes his patient back to the days of childhood traumas. Al Habsi's idea was to have him speak of his recent days in exile, his training, his comrades; to describe the rebels' organization, to reveal their plans; to talk of these things as if he was discussing them with his own companions, before he came back to Oman.

But Al Habsi had miscalculated. With rapt eyes and a foolish face the fellow opened his mouth and talked—profusely, in the present tense—about his days on the mountain. Then: "I must

167

go," he suddenly said, eerily. "I am late. Khilfan will wonder where I am." The Khilfan in question had been killed a year and a half before. "He is waiting. . . ."

While Al Habsi made futile efforts to bring him up to date, Issa became more and more desperate about this rendezvous with the long-dead Khilfan. Muttering frantically how late he was, he raised himself from the bed and tried to make for the door—the irons on his legs hindered him, he adjusted his stride to their rhythm and tottered resolutely doorwards again—at the iron-barred grill, while we watched him with paralysed fascination, he seized the bars and gave them a wrench which brought Al Habsi and I to our feet in fright. His strength under the drug was superhuman; and his obsolete urgency gave it a ghastly desperation.

"The cave, the cave, Khilfan is at the cave," he wailed, terribly : "I must go to Khilfan's cave. . . ."

That was all we ever got out of him. Bitterly bemoaning his inability to reach Khilfan and his cave, Issa eventually subsided into sleep, from which he awoke after a few hours as sane, and as resolutely lying, as he had been before the experiment. Al Habsi sagely shook his head. "I gave him too much," he regretted. "He went back too far." I shuddered, wondering what a really large overdose would do to a man, and forbade any mention of the devastating medicine again.

Al Habsi had other weird tricks in his repertoire. He was an adept at the sand-table. This is a way of divining the future, originally by means of a table on which sand is sprinkled and consulted by doodling apparently random lines and dots. But Al Habsi was modern; he used a pen and paper. Every now and again, while we were discussing the most ordinary things in my office, a dreamy look came over his face and he pulled out his fountain pen and reached for a piece of paper and inscribed copious lines and dots while staring glass-eyed at the ceiling. When he had done enough of this he looked down at the paper and went through what can only be described as a process of arithmetic. He added the symbols up, he subtracted them; for all I know he performed differential calculus with them. When he had done his sums he had produced, in a kind of unimaginable Q.E.D., an answer, which looked to me like just so many more lines and dots. Al Habsi then went to a locked box which he kept always with him and took out a yellow crumpled book which was the key to his Sybilline logarithms. After a few minutes of meditation he closed the book with a smile, winked at me, locked it up again, and carried on with the conversation as though nothing had intervened. He never told me what it was all about, nor, despite my pleadings, did he ever initiate me into the secrets of the sand-table. I am probably happier not to know.

During these days, too, the intelligence branch bore fruit, slowly at first, but with a self-seeding effect, and Jalali filled up as rapidly as our files.

The D.I.O. at Nizwa, a young man of unnatural thinness with a jaw like an Easter Island statue, achieved the biggest success of this intoxicating time. For months running into years, we had been hearing of the Oman Army of Liberation, a corps devoted to the invasion of Oman from a base in Saudi Arabia. Reports from the consulates, couched in diplomatically non-committal terms, told of the same bellicose enterprise. But so impossible was it to get acquainted in any palpable way with this spectral army that we all tended to regard it as a figment of either Talib's fancy or our own—or even the secret service's.

Then one day a crudely typewritten report, of many crumpled sheets, found itself on my desk at Bait-al-Falaj. It was the Nizwa D.I.O.'s weekly offering. And it featured a comprehensive exposé of the Oman Liberation Army. Like the Nazis with Cicero, we were so dazzled by this revelation that at first—and for some time—we regarded it as a red herring or even a leg-pull: I contributed to this devaluation, because it was such rich intelligence that incredulity was a reflex reaction.

We had been caught before by just such a tantalizing dish. The I.O. of the Trucial Oman Scouts once interviewed a man purporting to be one of Suleiman bin Himyar's slaves, who gave him no less than a complete dossier on the whole rebel organization in Oman. Every town of any size was laid bare: against each was a list of names a page long, with the address of traitorous houses and an inventory of their nefarious contents:

169

"Ibri: such-and-such a quarter, opposite mosque: house of so-and-so, servant of Talib; contains mines, hand grenades, and bombs". A colossal operation was mounted: simultaneously, at Awabi, Rostaq, Nizwa, Ibri, and as many other places as we had men to spare for, houses were identified, surrounded, and ransacked: the inhabitants, as many as we could find, were rounded up and put to the question. After we had spent a great deal of time, energy, and petrol we reached the inescapable conclusion that the whole thing was either a hoax or a mistake: the people we arrested were innocent of any treasonable crime; the houses we pillaged were empty of the smallest bomb; we found not so much as a suggestive letter. Who the informer was and what was his motive, remained for ever obscure to us. But we resolved never to be caught that way again.

So the Nizwa report seemed, to our resistant minds, a little too good to be true. As it circulated from office to office, from Maxwell to Smiley to Waterfield, it was garnished with glosses like "very interesting" or "quite so" and was quietly filed away. Only my patient clerk worked on at it, recording all the names dutifully on cards in a cabinet.

Then one day the lid blew off our complacency. The D.I.O. dug up a trio of Talib's recruits who were home on leave. He took them to his house on the outskirts of Nizwa; he fed them coffee, won their confidence, and eased out of them a full and free confession. Without so much as "I told you so" he sent this, poker-faced, to Bait-al-Falaj, where we blinked at it. Thereafter we rapidly learned as much about the Omani Liberation Army as we knew of our own. Throughout the ensuing months we ticked them off the muster roll, one by one, as we caught them and talked to them and let them go. Talib operated a press-gang in the oil-fields where so many Omani youths had gone to work, and most of these reluctant rebels were heartily glad to be out of the running. Some of them became agents for our intelligence. The threatened invasion never came.

In these days, too, we solved the Enigma of Al Qasayer. For years we had been plagued by the man. The Trucial Oman Scouts sent us regular notes on the activities of the dreaded

Shorty, reporting him here, there, and all over the place, his Land-Rover turning up at tedious intervals in a variety of colours anywhere between Abu Dhabi and Nizwa. The name of this peripatetic Pimpernel monopolized the intelligence reviews. The Al Qasayer who moved so magically through the T.O.S. reports, the Al Qasayer who was the doyen of mine-layers, obsessed us. As a further embellishment, the name of Grock—dear toothless Grock, Governor of Buraimi—was dragged protesting into the play. Al Qasayer, it was said, visited Grock at night. Grock was a confidant of Al Qasayer. Al Qasayer even used Grock's Land-Rover. The Scouts began to press for the removal of my comical old friend.

It was with the implication of Grock that the mystery solved itself. I recalled my days at Buraimi; I remembered asking Grock for a contractor, for a man to dig out our ill-favoured well . . . I remembered the mud-coloured man of gnomish stature who made himself so useful to us. Grock's bailiff. "Shorty" to his friends.

There had always been two Al Qasayers. The one who was seen all over the Trucial States and northern Oman was Grock's bailiff, pursuing his lawful business in one or another of the Government Land-Rovers, which were of different colours. The one who was believed to lay every mine in Oman was somebody else; and he, we learnt later, had never set foot in Oman since the capture of the Jebel Akhdhar. The chronicle of Al Qasayer came to an ignominious close, and his file was relegated to the archives.

We were slowly clambering on top of the problem.

I had one advantage over officers wrestling with similar jobs in other parts of the world. I held—metaphorically—the keys of Jalali. I needed no conviction in any court of law before consigning a man to its dungeons. For the Sultanate of Muscat and Oman recognized only orthodox Islamic law, and this derives entirely from the Koran. The Koran was compiled some thirteen centuries ago, and makes no mention of laying mines or harbouring explosives or any of the crimes which we were now pursuing. There would have been no point in arraigning our captives before any court, because they had committed no Koranic crime.

We therefore had no choice but to incarcerate them without trial. The authorities in Muscat were enthusiastically co-operative. I had only to dispatch one of my victims to the Interior Ministry with a note saying, "this is so and so, he is a layer of mines," for the doors of Jalali to swallow him up for evermore. This saved everybody a great deal of trouble.

By now the Gendarmerie, too, was in full cry. Its driving force was a pistol-packing Palestine policeman with a zest for arrest called Carl Seton-Browne, and with him and his gendarmes tightening their grip on the northern approaches the leaks were steadily being sealed up. Seton-Browne was a hairy-faced professional policeman, unlike the rest of us who were mostly amateur soldiers, and his methods derived from his days as a scourge of terrorists in pre-Israel Palestine. What these methods were I never found out, but they had a spectacular effect. The whole of his precinct was petrified.

Mines still filtered through, however; mines still blew us up. The big holes were bunged but it was like plugging a sieve. The big agents were cast into Jalali, but there were others, less conspicuous. The big mine-layers were put out of the way, or warned off by their friends when the hue and cry went up, but there were innumerable smaller fry. For example, there was Salem Mohammed and Rashid al Siyabi, perhaps the most improbable pair of saboteurs who ever handled a bomb.

Salem Mohammed was just a name in our card index. He came from Sharaija, Suleiman bin Himyar's capital, and he had served him during the rebellion as a bodyguard. After the flight from the Jebel Akhdhar he had followed Suleiman to exile and continued in his service.

And now the soldiers had arrested a man with a rifle: for twentieth century firearms were forbidden. He had been identified as one Salem Mohammed. The report which accompanied him to Bait-al-Falaj said, further, that he had come back home bearing mines together with an adherent of Saleh bin Issa called Rashid al Siyabi. I searched my files in vain for a mention of this man; he was a new star. But the account of the explosive ambitions of this pair was reliable, if uncorroborated. Its author was one of the D.I.O.'s converted rebels, who had played stool-pigeon in the guard-room with Salem. I had no reason to doubt it.

When I saw Salem Mohammed I shrank from the prospect of interrogating him. Of middle age and dwarfish stature, he had a head much too big for him and an expression of the most irresistible charm. He smiled on me indulgently when we met, called down the blessings of Allah upon me, hoped with limpid sincerity that I was well and asked me for a cigarette.

Until the leaders took him to Dammam he had scarcely ever left the cloud-rimmed plateau of the Jebel Akhdhar : once or twice a year he would bound down to Nizwa market for domestic reasons, and loped back up again to home. As Omanis were aloof from the rest of Arabia, so Salem was remote from the relatively cosmopolitan cities of the Oman plain. He was as simple as a child; but he had a sort of unclouded wisdom that derived from the very roots of nature. I and he were as far apart, as incomprehensible the one to the other, as an eagle and a snail. And I had to interrogate him.

The first, and hardest, task was to penetrate his preternatural good will, an abounding benevolence which seemed a relic from before the Fall of Man. How to get him to realise our respective rôles, of indicated traitor and vengeful inquisitor, was a conundrum. He just beamed upon me, made not the smallest complaint about his shackles nor his cell, and quite obviously could not understand why I was asking all these questions.

But nor did he answer any of my questions, in any way satisfactory to me. His fealty was to his chief, and he had no obligations to the inquisitive infidel who was trying for reasons known only to himself to pry into the affairs of the King of Nebhania. Our first interview ended in frustration for me and mystification for Salem Mohammed.

As our acquaintance ripened, he began to talk more expansively, but never to any real point. He agreed that he had been one of Suleiman's bodyguard. He recounted to me, like an old soldier entertaining a young admirer, some anecdotes from those heroic times. Yes, he nodded encouragingly, he was with Suleiman in exile. But he had grown weary of the foreign climate, and asked to retire, which had been granted him. He had accordingly made his harmless way homewards, where unaccountably, but doubtless it was the will of the Almighty, he had been seized by soldiers and made captive. He hoped, but did not make too much of it, that I or my superiors would soon send him home. Oh yes, he recalled, his travelling companion had been one Rashid al Siyabi, whom he had met on the way and from whom he had parted on arrival in Oman. Mines, he wagged his head solemnly, he had never heard of such things. His rifle? He had been given it by a friend.

The next step was obvious. I could make no headway with this son of Nature until I had quizzed his comrade Rashid al Siyabi, and eventually confronted them with each other in the classic method of the French magistracy. I sent for Rashid al Siyabi. He was found peaceably milking some goats in his brush-wood home, and he had apparently no blain on his conscience : in he came on his own two feet.

I had been expecting a break-through via Rashid al Siyabi, but I quickly abandoned my hopes. This was an elderly man of woolly intellect and ruminant features : a bi-pedal sheep. He greeted me with a meaningless grin, which never changed its alignment or lost its saliva-garnish from the moment I saw him to the day we said farewell, a period of some four weeks. Rashid al Siyabi filled me with no more optimism than had the intelligent but super-simple Salem.

Rashid al Siyabi was perfectly straightforward. Grinning damply he made it quite clear that he had brought no mines with any Salem Mohammed. He had never seen, nor heard mention of, anybody of that name. Furthermore, so far from having brought mines from Saleh bin Issa, he had not so much as heard the word "mine" in his life. He had not recently returned from abroad, with or without Salem Mohammed. He had not returned from anywhere. He had never been anywhere in his life, ever. He leered like a satyr. His breath was miasmal.

I gained not an inch beyond this point, by talking to the maddening pair separately, so I decided to see what happened if I had them both in together. In they came : Salem Mohammed blessing me solemnly, with raised hand and warm heart; Rashid

174

al Siyabi chewing a moist cud. They looked at each other. "How are you, my friend?" asked Salem Mohammed. "Who are you?" asked Rashid. They sat down, each with his fettered feet folded under him, on the floor. Salem nodded politely at the discomfited Rashid, who pulled theatrically puzzled faces to show that he was mystified by Salem's recognition.

The conversation hobbled along in a limp-legged way until I casually dropped the word, "Jalali". Jalali, I mused aloud; Jalali was a place where I was wont to send those who displeased me; those who, for example, told me lies, for I had a virtuous abhorrence of falsehood and felt a divine urge to chastise it. Rashid merely drooled at me but Salem turned on him and told him with some heat not to be more of a fool than nature had made him. If Rashid wanted to go to Jalali, said Salem, that was nobody's business but his own; but Salem was damned if Rashid was going to take him with him. Why, he asked him with passion, deny that they had travelled home together? I chose this moment to dismiss Salem and concentrate on the unhappy Rashid, by now cringing.

Having convinced Rashid that I had heard all about his travels, I turned the screw another notch. "Mines," I told him. "Mines?" he repeated vaguely. "Mines, Salem has told me about your mines. Salem," I went on, "is a sensible man. Salem is going home soon. He has told me all about you and your mines, and he will be well rewarded. You," I concluded, "you, on the other hand, will go shortly to Jalali. Unless, of course, you choose to be helpful too."

There followed several days of this. I interviewed them at tedious length, together, separately, in turns; by night and day, in their cells and in my office. I loosed Al Habsi on them, severally and together. I threatened, and applied, more persuasive treatment: they were tied hand and foot; they were denied cigarettes; they were left alone to meditate for solitary days on end. By a prolonged barrage of inquisition I at long last broke down Salem's honest reticence and Rashid's devious idiocy. They accused each other with enthusiasm. I had by now gauged their characters sufficiently to know that Salem was a truthful man as far as he chose to go, and that Rashid was almost compulsively mendacious in every word he uttered. This helped me to assess their depositions.

The story as it finally emerged, piecemeal and jumbled, was this. Salem, pining for his mountains from the exiles' palace, wanted to go home. He formed up to Suleiman bin Himyar and made his request. Suleiman said he could go, provided that he took some mines with him and blew somebody up when he got to Oman. Pleading age, infirmity, and ignorance, Salem protested; but his sheikh was adamant. Salem compromised. He would lay any number of mines, if he was supplied with them inside Oman, but he absolutely declined to run the risk of smuggling them in. Suleiman eyed him shrewdly, snapped his fingers at a slave, and sent for one of the sons of Harib bin Saif al Bida'i who was still at large and who happened to be there. Harib's son, explained the mountain chief, knew where there were abundant mines, safely within the frontiers of Oman. Harib's son would accompany Salem; Salem would collect them; Harib's son would return, and Salem would go on his way, laying his mines en route.

"Done," said Salem, and the two of them set out by dhow for Dubai and home.

On the way they were joined by Rashid al Siyabi, who had never been one of the stars of the rebel movement at all but had simply been hanging around Saleh bin Issa hoping for a job. No job had materialized, so he too was making his way homewards. The ill-matched trio landed at Dubai and caught a lift to Sohar. The Harib encampment was just south of Sohar, and nearby was a date grove. Leaving Salem and Rashid under a tree, the son of Harib went off to the date grove. He returned after dark, and with him was a donkey, four anti-tank mines as big as soup tureens, a modern rifle and an old breech-loader. Bidding them farewell, the lad vanished into the night.

Salem and Rashid set out foot-slogging down the main coast road, the explosive-burdened beast between them; they passed, no doubt, many military patrols and Government check points, but nobody gave a second glance at a solemn large-headed little man, his inane-looking companion, and their laden donkey.

Rashid's family lived among some lava hills about twenty

miles from Muscat, and for the sake of companionship Salem went with Rashid as far as his hills, intending to join the main Muscat-Nizwa road. As they neared the black crinkled rocks they began to argue.

"What are we going to do with these mines?" asked Salem.

"Eh?" said Rashid.

"We're not going to lay these mines, are we? I want to get home, and stay there in peace. If you want them you can have them."

"Yes," said Rashid. "I want the rifle too."

"You can't have the rifle and the mines," said Salem. "Or if you do, then I keep the donkey. And what do you want with the mines?"

"Want the rifle," persisted Rashid.

"I," said Salem firmly, "am keeping the rifle. I need it on the Jebel Akhdhar; there are wolves. What do you want with it down here? Besides, you can't shoot."

"I'll tell about your mines if I don't get the rifle."

"And you'll end up in the same place as me."

"I want the rifle."

They quarrelled about the rifle for the last two days of their journey together. In the end they reached agreement. Salem would take the rifle. Rashid would keep the breech-loader, the donkey—and the mines. Rashid's eyes gleamed. Salem parted from him and made for the main road. Bearing his rifle proudly, he marched up the highway homewards; but a military patrol stopped him, seized his incriminating weapon, arrested him and packed him off to Nizwa. There he was identified; the D.I.O.'s stool-pigeon chatted with him in the cells; and here he was, apologetic but unashamed.

Rashid had meanwhile woken up to his predicament. He was safely at home, with a donkey and a gun; but he was also saddled with four great green mines, which he had no more idea how to operate than he had of driving a bus, and which were a certain one-way ticket to Jalali if found. In panic, he told his brother, who by all accounts was a more responsible creature than Rashid. Big brother took the mines away, further into the hills, and buried them. Rashid stayed at home, goat-minding, until the summons from authority reached him; and here, too, was he, abject and anxious to make amends.

I sent Salem home, as his guilt was negligible; and he got his rifle back.

The problem now was to lay our hands on the mines, to which Rashid held the clue. Rashid was even more obtuse and obstructive over this than he had been over his initial interrogation. He even had to go into Jalali for a while; a chastening experience. Twice we sent small patrols to areas indicated by Rashid, and found not the smallest trace of a mine. At last I divined the truth; the poor fellow was scared stiff of his brother; if the soldiers went straight to the spot, Brother would know who had directed them, and unimaginable consequences would flow. Rashid was writhing on the horns of a prickly dilemma. I rescued him by calling off the military and sending in my tame sorcerer Al Habsi to mesmerize the brother, accompanied by one of Rashid's tribal chiefs to lend him authority. And at last, one fine afternoon, in came Al Habsi, bearing triumphantly four ferocious-looking mines. After a salutary interval Rashid was released from Jalali and sent home with a caution.

Carl Seton-Browne descended with his gendarmes on Harib's date-grove, and dug it up from edge to edge. They found, under a young date-palm, a hole where something had been concealed in sacking : nothing more.

And that was the end of that.

16

WHO BLEW UP FATHER CHRISTMAS?

"WELCOME aboard," said a briny voice. From somewhere near at hand, as I heaved myself awkwardly up a swaying ladder, the tooth-aching tones of a bo'sun's pipe scraped up and down a nautical arpeggio. As I regained my balance I glanced at the musician. He was an elderly scrawny Arab dressed in a blue checked loin-cloth, a white towel round his head, and little else of note. Then I looked at the officer standing arthritically at attention with his hand to his hat in a naval salute. It was Jasper, Grand Admiral of His Highness's Fleet. I was calling on him aboard his flagship.

"Mind your nut on the deck-head," Jasper's salt-caked voice steamed on. "Just step down the companion-way and we'll go aft to the wardroom." Jasper wore a white yachting cap, and the metamorphosis from Group Captain—via Sultan's standard-bearer and Jasper's Horse—into master mariner was obviously complete. That his ship was a rusty motor-launch, his ship's company two or three dhow-scrapers and a lascar bo'sun who had learnt to pipe on the East India Station, detracted not a jot from the pride of his bearing nor the flavour of his speech. The sea-change had been thorough.

We settled ourselves tightly into the captain's cabin, which was also wardroom and shipwright's locker. Jasper poured pink gins—the sun was, I noticed, over the yard-arm—and related tales of the sea. Lunch arrived : a mess of Arab pottage, fish and rice and an eloquent sauce. "Want to go to the heads?" asked Jasper.

179

Jasper's hospitable pink gins suggested that I did, and the heads were my next port of call. They were a primeval lavatory bowl with a complex appurtenance of pipes and pumps, taps and cocks, which needed to be addressed in the right order to achieve evacuation and avoid disaster. I nearly tripped over the outfall on my way back to the wardroom, where I found Jasper in convocation with his bo'sun and some charts. Jasper, it seemed, could interpret Admiralty charts, even if his sailing-master could not. He had buckets of the things stowed all round his cabin, and liked nothing better than to take them out and navigate all over them.

Jasper was in clover. There had always been an indefinable something about him that smacked of the sea; and now he smacked of the sea from the tip of his white cap to the toes of his plimsolls. He spent his days beating up and down the coast of Oman, deterring gun-runners, putting heart into far-flung governors, making friends with fishermen. Sometimes the Medical Officer would accompany him; a hilarious Indian doctor who looked and conducted himself like Punch. This waggish man of science traversed the land with a medical-looking black bag containing phials of the elixir of love. Whenever Jasper put him ashore at some long-lost fishing village he was immediately surrounded by a clamorous throng of distressed old men who had recently espoused nubile wives whom they found hard to oblige. They milled anxiously around the doctor's black bag, making pathetic gestures with their little fingers to demonstrate their particular woe. Doctor, licking his lips, opened his bag and went to work. Choosing a deliberately blunt needle he charged it full with his philtre, jammed the instrument home, and ground it around inside the patient's flesh before withdrawing it. This way, he assured me, the sufferers were convinced of the efficacy of his medicine. A painless injection, a tasteless drug, a gentle aperient were objects of scorn among these hairy hypochondriacs: the jab had to hurt, the physic to nauseate; the cathartic must be positively volcanic before they thought they had been treated at all. So the medico pandered to their whim. He made sure his needle was felt. When his surgery was finished, the hills were alive with frolicking old men, skipping like young goats over the horizon to home. The prescription must have worked, because there was always an enthusiastic crowd awaiting him wherever he landed. What it was I never found out; like Al Habsi's Truth Drug, this love potion is an Arabian mystery.

The last I saw of Jasper was one misty morning after I had been accompanying him on a combined exercise with one of Her Majesty's frigates. Jasper, to the huge amusement of the blue-jackets, had scrounged from the sail-maker and carpenter and shipwright an astonishing miscellany of stores: beeswax, sail-cloth, holy-stone and tar. With these he delightedly returned to his own tight ship, after a plenitude of pink gins; the frigate steamed away and Jasper set his course for Tiwi or some other improbably-named port of call.

As the sleek grey man-of-war slid towards the horizon Jasper suddenly remembered that he had forgotten something: a belaying-pin, a marline-spike, a foretop-gallant or even some pink gin; whatever it was, it demanded the urgent recall of the fast-vanishing warship. Jasper climbed on top of the deck-house, wrapped his feet securely around the rudimentary mast, and began frantically to signal—his hairy arms, before my fascinated gaze, commenced a fluent oration in semaphore. There was a long, awed silence from the frigate. Then at last the Yeoman of Signals must have dredged down into the depths of his boyhood training and realized what these demented limbs purposed. An Aldiss lamp winked back, in respectful acknowledgement. Jasper—his feet by now entwined almost inextricably about his mast—wagged his arms with determination and the dialogue continued to a dignified close. Her Majesty's Ship hove to, Jasper beat up to her, the transfer of nautical necessities took place, the man-of-war gave Jasper a hoot of homage and the grand old man of the sea chugged home.

For the remainder of my service in Oman I was fully absorbed in intelligence. And the pattern we unfolded became more and more complex. The original problem had been straightforward, if intractable: Talib in Dammam was sending his men into Oman to plant mines. That was all there was to it. All we had to do was find out who these gentry were, and catch them: each one, when caught, revealed a little more about his colleagues, and made it a little easier to intercept the next party.

But slowly, as my files filled up, a new element became increasingly clearly discernible. There had been incidents which seemed unusual, even in the abnormal setting of Oman. Father Christmas, the patriarchal Minister of the Interior, was blown up one day. He was aboard a British India liner, en route for a holiday in India. On his first night at sea he capriciously decided that he preferred to sleep with his feet on the pillow and his head at the foot of the bunk : why, apart from the divine influence, remains an enigma. At any rate, he had composed himself to sleep in this inverted fashion, when there was a shattering explosion and the cabin filled with smoke and fumes. His feet were flayed and slightly grilled, but he was otherwise unhurt. The ensuing investigation adduced that a time bomb had been placed under his pillow, and had it not been for his unaccountable whim he would have been killed.

Then there was the case of the missing air liner, which called up Sharjah ten minutes before landing and was never seen or heard again. This remained a complete mystery until reports from Dammam told us of two well-known saboteurs who had boarded the plane for Sharjah bearing with them a time bomb in their baggage. To their presumed disgust, quite apart from the tragedy to the rest of the plane-load, they had miscalculated the time of flight and the bomb went off in mid-air.

The good ship *Dara,* another of the unfortunate British India liners, blew up at sea off Dubai, caught fire and sank, with the loss of several hundred souls. The evidence there pointed directly to a time bomb. Another time bomb went off on the deck of the equally good ship *Dwarka*, also a B.I. boat (and furthermore the one where Father Christmas had had his alarming experience).

Bangs in Muttrah, the landward suburb of Muscat, were becoming a commonplace. Mines, for the first time in history, were heard from Bait-al-Falaj, far away from the stamping-ground of Talib's operators, and, uncharacteristically, they were laid on a road that was in constant use by civilian lorries. A bomb exploded in the postal sorting office in Bahrein, of all places, in a parcel addressed to the Sultan's private secretary. One of the Sultan's Air Force aeroplanes was sabotaged by cotton waste stuffed into its petrol tank—fortunately discovered before doing any damage.

Most of these strange phenomena could not be accounted for as easily as a mine on the Izki road. Salem Mohammed, Rashid al Siyabi, and the rest could scarcely be imagined planting time-bombs in state-rooms of ocean liners, or scuttling aeroplanes. There was a more sophisticated organization now at work. The question was, was it run by Talib; or was it independent? If the latter, was it allied with him, or was it antipathetic? As it was hard to imagine Talib's fanatical Saracens blowing up ships, so it was impossible to imagine any conspiracy sophisticated enough to sabotage aircraft, being in the least bit anxious to see a return of the Imamate.

The Sultan was reactionary enough for most people. He forbade smoking, except in private, throughout his domains. The British Consul-General was once a guest in his palace, which was served by a sanitary system as elaborate as it was strange. The Consul was exploiting the seclusion of his privy one morning in order to snatch a quick drag; he threw the cigarette-end into the hole, where a never-ending stream bore it away. But he had not been back in his room more than a few moments when a big black slave knocked and entered, and in his hands was a silver salver, and on the salver was a soggy cigarette-end. The Consul was given to understand that if it had not been caught in time it would have ended up in the Sultan's quarters, and a diplomatic incident would have developed.

But at least the Sultan was living in the Middle Ages. The Imamate was still embalmed in the days of the Prophet. Where the Sultan was reviled by his urban subjects for being a medieval Caliph, he was anathematized by the adherents of the Imam for being only one step short of Iblis himself : he was so modern, so tainted with secularism, that the holy men of the interior looked upon him as the crowned heads of Europe regarded Robespierre and Lenin. The Sultan was walking a tight-rope; and Blondin-like he maintained his balance.

We scratched our heads and wondered what this paradoxical new threat might be. I had been hearing for some time about a secret political party, alleged to number among its membership some highly notable characters in Muscat and on the coast, and which was reputed to be crypto-communist by persuasion. I had a list of names of those supposed to belong to this party, who met secretly at night and plotted: was this party genuine, and if so was it subversive or merely disputatious? And if subversive, was it responsible for the new threat? I sifted and filtered the crude lumps of raw intelligence and extracted filmy wisps of fact. Out of the dust emerged one name, time and time again, like a theme in a symphony. Abdulmajid. As soon as I realized that this man was news, I burrowed through the card index to see what I could find. There was hardly anything. He had been one of Talib's lieutenants on the Jebel Akhdhar during the campaign: he had been wounded, and had henceforth withdrawn from public life. When last heard of he was setting himself up in business in Bahrein.

He was, however, on our black list. The black list was a tally of all those who were due for Jalali without further ado should they ever fall into our hands. Abdulmajid was no mere liberation army recruit: he was a mutinous sheikh. He had, we presumed, no wish to see the inside of Jalali.

While I was compiling evidence against this interesting business man, his references on our card index proliferated. Abdulmajid, I learnt, was a home-loving man; prosperous though his Bahrein business was, the burden of perpetual exile lay achingly upon him. Abdulmajid wanted to come home; or at least he wanted his family to join him. Abdulmajid's family were wards of the Sultan, domestic hostages, and were as unable to travel to join him in Bahrein as he was to return to their bosom at home.

Abdulmajid's cousin and best friend was Zahar, Saif's old crony at Rostaq.

The plot began to set. Abdulmajid was our man.

I took to spending whole days in the area of Rostaq, calling on as wide a selection of the populace as I could, in order to conceal, among the multitude I attended, the fact that I was consulting with one particular sheikh. For Zahar's association with me was of no use whatever unless it was disguised. So I coffeed with the Governor, with sycophantic aristocrats, with innumerable lesser citizens, to my utter tedium. The outcome of this offensive was that Zahar took a few days off from home and made a trip to Dubai, expenses paid; on some domestic pretext or other.

About ten days afterwards I was sitting in my quarter at Bait-al-Falaj listening to my gramophone when there was a delicate knock on my door and in crept Zahar. He had made contact with Abdulmajid, he told me, excited as a child. He showed me a letter, a noncommittal note, which I kept until I was able to compare its handwriting with a specimen we had of Abdulmajid's correspondence from the days of the Jebel Akhdar. It was genuine.

Another exchange of letters followed, and the next time I met Zahar—at Rostaq this time—he produced a letter in an elaborate cipher. In this Abdulmajid expatiated on his yearning for his family but pointed out that there were enough examples languishing in Jalali of people who had accepted in good faith invitations to return to Oman, to make him undesirous of coming home. He demanded for his family passports and safe conduct out of Oman to join him in Bahrein where he intended to settle. As a gesture of goodwill he included in a postscript the name of the perpetrator of a recent bomb outrage, a name we had elicited by other means but which betokened Abdulmajid's bona fides.

I had then to persuade Father Christmas to consider the question of the family: a wife and one or two little boys. Permission in principle was granted. The next letter to Abdulmajid laid down the conditions: he must deliver to us the complete organization which was responsible for the new developments on the terrorist front: the sophisticated conspiracy which put bombs in ships and aeroplanes and Muttrah streets; which mined the main roads around Muscat; which put bombs in parcels in Bahrein.

My comprehensive terms were delivered to Abdulmajid via Zahar's code and false addresses. Swiftly the answer came back. Zahar was to visit Abdulmajid in Bahrein, where the whole deal would be discussed between them. I arranged for Zahar to travel

185

to Bahrein, and then, to save time, to report back to the officer in charge of military intelligence at British Army headquarters there. Off he went.

By coincidence, the District Intelligence Officer from Nizwa—that cliff-jawed young man who had broken into the Oman Liberation Army—was on leave in Bahrein. Walking past the I.O.'s house one evening he spotted my friend, squatting patiently outside on the pavement waiting to report after his visit to Abdulmajid. He engaged him in conversation; Zahar told him all; imaginatively seizing the initiative, the Nizwa D.I.O. thereupon hailed a taxi and together they drove off to talk turkey with Abdulmajid.

Abdulmajid turned out to be a pasty-faced owlish man in glasses, young and plump and conceited. He pushed up the stakes. He now no longer wanted his family, he said; the unexplained release of the Sultan's hostages would expose him as an informer. He wanted a perpetual safe custody; signed and sworn by the Minister of the Interior. He wanted an amnesty for himself and certain associates. And he wanted twenty thousand pounds in cash. For this, he said modestly, he would blow the lid off the entire organization.

In the course of the conversation the D.I.O. had subtly extracted from Abdulmajid a number of names which were more or less germane to the conspiracy under discussion, but Abdulmajid refused to be drawn further. Twenty thousand pounds, he said, and we could have it all in our laps. Nor was he concerned with haggling. Bahrein was booming, his business was doing well, and the hundred rupee notes we used so effectively in Oman were so much waste paper to him. Twenty thousand pounds might seem small enough beer to a Bahrein merchant but it made the starved exchequer of Muscat wince. They said an aghast, "No." I began to marvel at the monster I had raised; the whole affair had moved rapidly out of my class. I returned gratefully to the simple level of my Rostaq friend, and discussed with Zahar what we had learnt. It turned out to be considerable. I had the list of names the D.I.O. had slipped out of Abdulmajid, and they were more significant than the merchant can have thought : comparing them with my files, I found they tallied uncannily with what I had patiently accumulated from here and there about the supposed political party. The sophisticated conspiracy existed, and we were hard on its trail. There was a bank clerk in Qatar (where a bomb had recently gone off in the strongroom); there was a trader in Kuwait; there were some brothers also in Kuwait, with other brothers in Muscat and elsewhere; Dubai had its share. All these people were members of the extremely small class of educated Omanis (the Sultan had always regarded education with the same distaste he had for smoking). The few scholars who had managed to smuggle themselves an education were cordially hostile to the Sultan; they were also inspired by half-digested slogans of Arab nationalism, and were equally hostile to the British influence—in both these animosities they shared common cause with Talib, from whom they obtained mines and bombs. Both wanted the end of the Sultan and no more British. How they would get on together, ruling ancient Oman, was another question, which they had not yet found time to pose.

We wrote to Abdulmajid again, Zahar and I. We enclosed the safe conduct and the perpetual amnesty; and we enclosed a modest sum of money, as much as we could afford, and asked him to send us the one thing we so far lacked : the Muscat end of the plot. Sure enough, as the sound businessman he was, Abdulmajid gave us what he thought was value for money. Thinking we were still ignorant of the great external network, he sent us what to him was chicken feed : the local cells. He thus filled in our gaps. There was a man employed with the Sultan's air force; uniquely placed to stuff cotton waste into a petrol tank. There was a member of our own army in Bait-al-Falaj. There were, interestingly but unfortunately, others, illustrious enough in the Government and aristocracy of Muscat to make it unwise for us to pursue the matter more purposefully. But knowledge is strength, and at last they too knew that we knew. We were on level terms with the enemy who had for so long been a faceless nightmare.

At the end of 1961 I felt that I had been in Oman long enough. I applied for an appointment as a political officer in the Hadhramaut, which I thought would be a pleasant change after nearly five years of Omanis.

Of those I had known from the beginning, Eric Johnson had preceded me southward; Gunpowder Joe, Bob Warner and Jasper soldiered on in Muscat; Grock had peacefully died.

Early in the New Year my friends threw me a head-cracking party and poured me on to an aeroplane bound for Mukalla.

I was going to see some more of Arabia.

EPILOGUE

T H E six months after my departure was a time of triumph for the Sultan's men.

The troops of the garrison on top of the Jebel Akhdhar had been enduring for over a year their own private guerilla war. The rebels laid no mines up there, for there were no roads, but the tumbled chaos of rock and the great cliffs and gorges provided a splendid playground for a small but tough gang of mountain men who made a habit of ambushing the soldiers on patrol. There were no spectacular disasters, but the guerillas were a dangerous and perpetual nuisance and they hampered the work of reconstruction.

Then came the breakthrough. The Northern Frontier Regiment, after many attempts, managed to trap the ambushers, killing two and wounding a couple more. The gang leader and a notorious mine-layer were eliminated from the game. The lesson was sharp, and the ambushes stopped.

This small but decisive victory was followed in August by the capture of a dhow off the Batina coast. On board were two of the most eagerly-sought rebels in Talib's whole force; one was the man who had escaped from Nick Carter's Ibri ambush back in 1959, and who had since risen to the top of the list. The two leaders were accompanied by ten other much-wanted men and a large cargo of arms, mines, and other warlike stores. Interrogation of this rich prize led to the discovery and apprehension of some thirty other rebels and their sympathizers in Oman, and the seizure of some more lethal material.

Talib's network in the country reeled and collapsed under this blow, and never recovered. It was the end of the affair that had begun five weary years before. One or two bangs were heard afterwards, but they were unrelated to the Imam and his tire-some brother.

After the final calamity the scheming three in Dammam turned to diplomacy and international politics. With Talib conspicuous as always, they spent much of their own time and other people's money touring Arab capitals trying to drum up support for their grievances. The Arab League adopted their cause at the United Nations, which appointed two commissions to investigate their complaints. One of these parties visited Oman, and acquitted the Sultan of the charges of aggression which had been laid against him. The second commission, which was not invited to Oman, called for the withdrawal of British troops but failed to declare itself unreservedly in favour of the rebels. Most delegates to the United Nations found it hard to devote their full attention to the suit of Ghalib bin Ali, Imam of Oman, against Sayid Said bin Taimur, Sultan of Muscat and Oman, or to recognize it as anything more than a paltry squabble between a petty panjandrum and a pestilent priest.

The issue is not stone dead, but it is manifestly moribund; and with the recent discovery (in 1964) and current development of the oil which began the whole dispute, the people of the country themselves see it as increasingly irrelevant, a relic of their medieval history.

With the clearing of the attics in Oman Proper, the centre of gravity shifted to Dhofar, a remote province some eight hundred miles down the coast from Muscat which the Sultan maintained as his private domestic estate. In Dhofar he kept a personal army, entirely distinct and separate from the forces in Oman, and he was even more jealous of the inviolability of Dhofar to outside inquisitiveness than he was of Muscat's.

There was, however, an American oil company prospecting in the desert hinterland (which was allowed no liquor by his Highness), and a small R.A.F. staging post (which was permitted to drink). A certain incorrigible trouble-maker named Bin Nafl fell foul of the Sultan and assaulted an oil company truck, killing a Government guard. Bin Nafl fled across the sands to Saudi Arabia, and returned in the middle of 1964 bearing with him the now familiar souvenirs of such trips abroad, arms and mines. He used these to such effect that the Sultan's Armed Forces had to hasten to Dhofar—something previously unheard of. Bin Nafl's movement grew, with the enthusiastic assistance of the Iraqis, who trained his gangsters, and the ever-ready Egyptians who supplied him with the means. This part of the story has not yet closed, as I write.

Meanwhile, the face of Oman has changed. Where I once spent two days in anguish trying to reach Jasper at Sohar, there is now a good motor road of graded gravel all the way up the Batina coast. Medical dressing stations, which Talib once considered a suitable target for his time bombs, are now scattered liberally throughout the country. Where once the oil company Scammels ran the gauntlet of mines and bullets at Izki, there are now 270 miles of pipeline running all the way from the oil strikes to a terminal point and storage area near Bait-al-Falaj. Where once the only officers the Sultan had were the gallant but elderly Maxwells, Jaspers, and Warners, and the home-grown Ali Mohammeds, the return of his son and Crown Prince, Qabus, from Sandhurst infused professionalism into a keen but amateur force.

Slowly, but determinedly, Muscat and Oman is heaving itself out of the middle ages. We can only wish it well; but I am glad I knew it before the *aggiornamento*.